Praise for **A Book of Mormons**

"*A Book of Mormons* is a refreshing collection of brief essays from people of various stripes who relate their present or former encounters with Mormonism (and, in one instance, its sister tradition), not as it is preached from the pulpit or written in manuals and books, but as it is lived in the mundane world that most of us populate. Written neither to convert nor defend, and void of the truth claims that largely monopolized the first century-and-a-half of Mormon literature, the essays take us on a gentle journey that explores the simple, and yet increasingly relevant mantra of the modern Latter-day Saint: 'If it works, I stay.'"

–Gregory Prince, scholar and author of *David O. McKay and the Rise of Modern Mormonism*

"*A Book of Mormons* shows that the Mormon collective talent for first-person experience narratives and personal essays is alive and flourishing. A kind of literary step up from the 'I'm a Mormon videos,' this volume features diversity of a less visible sort as a range of thinkers describe—achingly, beautifully, and comically by turns—their dreams, labors, pains, and joys in building Zion."

–John Durham Peters is the A. Craig Baird professor of Communication Studies at the University of Iowa

A BOOK OF
MORMONS

A Note about the I Speak for Myself° series:

I Speak for Myself ® is an inclusive platform through which people can make themselves heard and where everyone's voice has a place. ISFM®'s mission focuses on delivering one core product, a "narrative collection," that is mindset-altering, inspiring, relatable, and teachable. We aim to deliver interfaith, intercultural titles that are narrow in scope but rich in diversity.

Please be sure to check out our website, www.ISpeakforMyself. com, to learn more about the series, join the conversation, and even create an I Speak for Myself ® book of your own!

Sincerely,

Zahra T. Suratwala and Maria M. Ebrahimji

Co-Founders, I Speak for Myself ®

BOOKS IN THE SERIES

Volume 1: *I Speak for Myself: American Women on Being Muslim*

Volume 2: *American Men on Being Muslim: 45 American Men on Being Muslim*

Volume 3: *Demanding Dignity: Young Voices from the Front Lines of the Arab Revolutions*

Volume 4: *Talking Taboo: American Christian Women Get Frank About Faith*

Volume 5: *Father Factor: American Christian Men on Fatherhood and Faith*

Volume 6: *Faithfully Feminist: Jewish, Christian, and Muslim Feminists on Why We Stay*

A BOOK OF MORMONS

Latter-day Saints on a Modern-Day Zion

edited by **Emily W. Jensen and Tracy McKay-Lamb**
foreword by **Janan Graham-Russell**

White Cloud Press
Ashland, Oregon

The views and opinions expressed by each contributing writer in this book are theirs alone and do not necessarily represent those of the series' editors or I Speak for Myself, Inc.

White Cloud Press books may be purchased for educational, business, or sales promotional use. For information, please write:

Special Market Department
White Cloud Press
PO Box 3400
Ashland, OR 97520
Website: www.whitecloudpress.com

Cover and interior design by Christy Collins, C Book Services
Cover photo provided by AJ Buruca Photography: http://www.ajburuca.com/
Interior images: Michael Austin, by Morris Thurston; Camille Fronk Olsen, courtesy of BYU

Printed in the United States of America
First edition: 2015
15 16 17 18 19   10 9 8 7 6 5 4 3 2 1

Library of Congress Cataloging-in-Publication Data
A book of Mormons: Latter-day Saints on a modern-day Zion / edited by Emily W. Jensen and Tracy McKay-Lamb ; foreword by Janan Graham-Russell.
    pages cm -- (I speak for myself series)
 Includes bibliographical references and index.
 ISBN 978-1-935952-90-9 (pbk. : alk. paper)
1. Zion (Mormon Church) 2. Christian life--Mormon authors. I. Jensen, Emily Warburton, editor. II. McKay-Lamb, Tracy, 1972- editor. III. Series: I speak for myself series.
 BX8643.Z55B66 2015
 289.3'32--dc23
                              2015031959

Dedication

To all those who seek for Zion,
may we discover it for our children.

Contents

Acknowledgements

We caught a small glimpse of Zion in compiling this book, as a diverse group of Mormons came together to produce something beautiful and timeless. We thank our writers, both for their brilliance and for the willingness to share themselves—through this very act, we embody our living faith. We thank the I Speak For Myself team for promoting the cause of community building and bettering through the personal stories of these contemporary Mormons. We thank our families, our respective ever-patient and hot husbands and our crazy and creative children for their patience and support.

Foreword

by Janan Graham-Russell

The baptismal waters were a passage, never fully parting from my life before, yet, unable to escape the future that lay ahead of me. In one space resided a heritage, a culture, a history—inescapable and life-affirming. The other, a culture known to me only through the words of missionaries. My journey is that of balance and navigating these spaces; the newfound identity as someone whose history is not in Zion. *How will I craft this narrative? How will I embrace my past with my present and future?* I will share with you what is perhaps one of my favorite stories I've heard in my years of writing; a story that continues to inspire me when I speak of those before me as I connect to them and them to me. The story begins as most stories do, with once upon a time.

Once upon a time there was a young woman. The woman had many homes but her favorite was a small blue house by the sea. In the nearby village, though the woman was admired for her bravery and wisdom, the villagers knew her the most for her travels. People came far and wide to the blue house to gaze upon the collection wondrous treasures and antiques from her adventures from all over the world. Swords from the greatest battles. Medallions for her bravery. Jewelry and china passed down to her. Everyone in the village marveled at the prosperity and wisdom of the woman.

Over time her bones grew thin as many do when twilight peers over the horizon. No longer in the days of her youth, she soon retreated from the small village and spent her days in the small house by the sea. Years passed and the triumphant stories of the woman became tales of legend and folklore. Villagers began to speculate as to what happened to the woman. Some said that all that was left in the house were dust and bones. Others said the house was haunted. One early evening, on a dare, a group of children from the village ventured to the house to see if the stories were true. No longer the vibrant blue of the earliest memories, the house was very much in disarray. With the strong winds approaching, one of the children jumped as the shutters groaned. "There's nothing here," one of the children said, disappointed. "Let's go back."

All the children followed. All but one.

Curious, the young girl opened the door. Beautifully made portraits lined the walls of this once-palace, only covering walls that had been stripped bare. The girl soon heard a creak. Frightened, she paused and placed her hands over mouth. She turned to her left, and in a chair was a woman staring out to the sea.

"I believe it is a story you are after," she sighed in a soft voice.

"Ya-ya yes," the girl stammered.

The woman let out a huff. "Well, you are the first to come here in years without running away. And I s'pose it is time I told someone."

The woman walked toward her bookcase and extended her hand for a book on the top shelf. "A bit weathered, like me," she laughed before she blew off the collection of dust.

The woman opened the book and began to craft the tales of her exploits. Traveling the world, dining with monarchs, great escapes from certain peril; the girl's eyes grew more and more wide as the woman described feats that stretched far beyond the realm of the young girl's imagination. Enamored by not only the stories themselves but how they were told, hours and hours went by. For a brief moment they heard the chiming of the grandfather clock. "It only rings at the right time," the woman chuckled. "It's getting late and I s'pose that someone will be worried about you." The girl sighed.

The woman rested her hand on the young girl's shoulder. "I think it is better that this goes with you. It's only collecting dust here."

The girl hesitated. "I couldn't. This is yours."

"If a ghost story could inspire you and your friends to come to this worn down shell, who knows what the truth will do," the woman replied, as she handed the book to the young girl. The girl nodded and slipped the book into her satchel. With book in tow, she ran back to the village.

We all have stories in our lives. Some stories speak of great adventures, some of overcoming our greatest fears, some of battles we have fought with others and within ourselves. Others, tales of faith and communion, heartbreak and desolation. It is important that we tell these stories, *our* stories, as they are our connection to one another and offer insight to our truest selves, revealing a bravery that we may not have recognized before. Often times, when others speak for us, they speak of ghost stories and folk tales about our lives. When those stories overcome those within us, they become the normal, the standard, and the spirit expires. In the following essays, you will read the narratives of those who refused to let that spirit expire. We travel from the mountains and valleys of faith, religion, history, culture to give us a glimpse of the power of the connections that our stories can build. With that, let us revel in our pasts, our presents, and our futures, because: who knows what the truth will do.

Introduction
by Emily W. Jensen and Tracy McKay-Lamb

Nice. Weird. Good. Odd. Smiley. Strange. Happy.

If you were to ask random people to define Mormons in a few words, you would likely get variations on those simple descriptors.[1]

This illustrates well the problem Mormons face in trying to define their religion in their own voice. Mormons are perceived generally as happy people whose strange American-born religion inspires them to be good, but it's still . . . weird. At least they are nice. And, some might whisper or wonder, perhaps a cult.[2]

With the advent of *The Book of Mormon* Broadway musical and Mitt Romney's failed presidency bids, the Mormon religion and its people have been in the modern spotlight. Interestingly, while the outside world has been attempting to uncover what makes Mormons Mormon, Mormons themselves have used this opportunity to redefine how their religion is viewed in the sometimes harsh light of contemporary views and values.[3] In attempting to be seen as "normal" instead of "weird" Mormons have sometimes downplayed their more unique doctrines.[4]

Enter Zion.

Zion is often associated with the Jewish faith, connected to the idea of a perfected Jerusalem. Mormon Church founder Joseph Smith latched onto this idea of a perfected city, an earthly home for the newly returned Jesus Christ. The details for this Mormon-themed Zion morphed from a geographically central place (first imagined in Missouri, then to some extent in Ohio and Illinois, and pushed westward into Utah[5]) to finally a more nebulous location as wherever Latter-day Saints "living with one heart and one mind" become a stake of Zion.[6] While a Zion city geographically platted out in Missouri was never fully realized, one can still sometimes find nostalgic yearnings for Zion in Mormon Sunday discourse, wrapped in speculative wondering about when we will all pioneer back to Independence, Missouri (the first city designated as Zion). Promises to live communally and care for one another are part of modern Temple worship, keeping Zion as a concept alive in the minds of contemporary Mormons. Finally, as outlined in this book, American Mormons, from a wide spectrum of beliefs, discuss what our unique and sometimes downplayed theological doctrine of Zion might mean today.

If you were to enter most any Mormon Church in America on the first Sunday of most months, you would hear Mormons standing at the pulpit, as directed by the Spirit, they explain, bearing their testimony on variations of this theme:

"I know the church is true. I know Joseph Smith was a true prophet and he restored church of Jesus Christ. I know we are led by a prophet today. I love my family. I am grateful that my Savior, Jesus Christ, died for me. The Spirit witnesses to me that this is true. In the name of Jesus Christ, Amen."

In the coming pages, you will also hear testimony—but testimony outside of the familiar pulpit language and cadence. Mormons are not a monolith, and they come from a variety of backgrounds with widely different life experiences. We have Mormons called to teach the youth at church, Mormon historians who study Zion for a living, Mormons who are Mormon because they love being Mormon and want to share that with the world, Mormon parents who struggle with the same parenting problems as most American parents, Mormons who are grappling with feminism, LGBQT issues, diversity, poverty, racism, depression, and more. John Hamer of the Community of Christ provides a small glimpse into another branch of the church Joseph Smith founded, and their comparable conceptualizations of Zion. We even have Mormons who have left the church, and some whom the church has left.

Zion will be defined and redefined in the coming pages. But most of all, Zion will be modeled. The idea that many individuals can come together, bringing their talents, their ideas, and even their disagreements to be discussed, is delightful, enriching, and inspiring.

Forget about glossy Mormon-produced documentaries. Forget about funny Broadway musicals. Forget about public relations and presidential campaigns. Here you will find a potent mixture of everyday and extraordinary Mormons speaking in their own voice about tough issues and hard-won testimonies. To truly understand who Mormons are in this modern age and to what they aspire, listen to us speak for ourselves.

Nice. Weird. Good. Odd. Smiley. Strange. Happy. All true, at times. Perhaps this collection of essays may add some depth to those simplified perceptions. Complicated. Nuanced. Thoughtful. Engaged. Faithful.

Zion.

NOTES

1. The Mormon Church would like outsiders to start by getting the name right, although there is a resignation that the Mormon moniker will be sticking around. The official name of the church is The Church of Jesus Christ of Latter-day Saints. For the purposes of this book, this official name, as well as Mormons, Mormon Church, LDS Church, and Latter-day Saints will all be used

2. No, says the official cult list of Billy Graham, who perhaps should not be the one making that distinction to the wider world, but regardless the Mormons were pretty happy to get off that list. See "Billy Graham No Longer Thinks Mormonism Is a Cult" (accessed 10/24/2014, http://newsfeed.time.com/2012/10/19/billy-grahamno-longer-thinks-mormonism-is-a-cult/).

3. Just recently the Mormon Church produced a documentary titled "Meet the Mormons" wherein much like this introduction, the narrator asked random New Yorkers what they knew about Mormons. Descriptors such as "racist" and "practices polygamy" and "doesn't dance" and "doesn't drink" were then given a figurative eye-roll as the movie went on to introduce some diverse and interesting Mormons who did not meet those stereotypes. However, that was a bit misleading, as those stereotypes have roots in prior practices that Mormons today are still unraveling. Besides this public relations piece, the Mormon Church leaders have also encouraged members to "flood the earth" with good gospel messages on social media. Thus Mormons are trying to put their best foot (tweets) forward and in doing so with such obedient missionary zeal, sometimes come off as naïve and insincere. See David A. Bednar's "To Sweep the Earth as with a Flood" (accessed November 15, 2014, https://www.lds.org/prophets-and-apostles/unto-all-the-world/to-sweep-the-earth-as-with-a-flood?lang=eng).

4. Two examples of unique doctrines deemed weird by others: a line designed to get laughs in the musical The Book of Mormon says "I believe that plan involved me getting my own planet," sings protagonist Elder Kevin Price, who later sings that "God lives on a planet called Kolob." Kolob is an idea that has been downplayed in recent years, and the church's current stance can be studied at "Becoming Like God" (accessed 10/24/2014, https://www.lds.org/topics/becoming-like-god?lang=eng). Another example is the idea of proxy baptisms for the dead that one sees in the news because some other religions find this practice offensive. For a current explanation on this unique doctrine see "Baptisms of the Dead" (accessed 10/24/2014, https://www.lds.org/topics/baptisms-for-the-dead?lang=eng).

5. This helps explain why there is a national park in Utah called Zion National Park.

6. See Moses 7:18, Pearl of Great Price. This will not be the last time you see this verse cited in the coming pages.

Building Zion: Folding Chairs
by Melissa Wei-Tsing Inouye

MELISSA WEI-TSING INOUYE was born and raised in Costa Mesa, California, by Warren and Susan Inouye and the members of the Costa Mesa First Ward. She earned her PhD in Chinese history from Harvard University in 2011. She, her husband, and their four children have previously lived in the People's Republic of China and in Hong Kong. They now reside in New Zealand, where Dr. Inouye is a lecturer in Asian Studies at the University of Auckland.

Personal names have been changed to protect people's privacy.

In Mormon scripture, the story of Enoch takes on a communal twist. In the Bible, it is just Enoch who is taken up to be with God; in Mormon scripture Enoch and the dwellers of his entire city are taken up into heaven.[1] The name of the city is Zion. When Latter-day Saints talk about "building Zion," therefore, the image of Zion as a shining city rising to heaven tends to flicker in the background. But when I think about "building Zion," the image in my mind is a yellow-brick meetinghouse with a dull gray spire on the corner of Placentia and Adams in Costa Mesa, California.

I was born and raised in Costa Mesa as a member of the Costa Mesa First Ward (*ward* is the Mormon term for a local congregation). Longtime members of the ward still remember my father standing at the back of the chapel, swinging my baby carrier back and forth in wide arcs to keep me quiet during the service. Some claim he used to loop-the-loop, but he denies this. Each Sunday my family went to church for three hours of worship and teaching. Various other activities also took place at the church building on other days of the week.

I spent good portions of my early childhood tearing around the Costa Mesa meetinghouse with my brothers like we owned the place. Our headquarters was the cultural hall, a large gym with basketball hoops and a raised stage flanked by plush curtains. The cultural hall hosted a wide range of events, from "ward socials" (seasonal parties) to "roadshows" (musical productions) to wedding receptions.

The organizing elements for these transformations were the folding tables and chairs, stored on long carts under the stage. As I child I observed how the folding and unfolding of tables and chairs (a quintessential Mormon activity) was both a science and an art. Not only could adult ward members haul heavy furniture with ease, they did so with little direction, telepathically discerning the next pressing collective task. Big carts were hauled out, the tables tipped on their sides, table legs pushed out and the braces slammed into position, the heavy metal chairs swung into place so that they unfolded in midair. I further observed that once this chair-setting-up—or taking-down—process was initiated by one person, everybody else sprang into action, like golden retrievers bounding irresistibly after a thrown stick. Over time, I too mastered the art of carrying multiple chairs in each hand and sensing the source from which the organizational vision flowed.

The ability to detect who was running each operation was important because Mormon congregations have no full-time professional clergy; church leadership changes regularly. Organizational roles ("callings") in a ward are filled by laypersons assigned or called to serve terms for an unspecified amount of time (in general, the terms range from one to seven years). At the ward level, people are called to positions by the bishop (the equivalent of a pastor or Catholic priest). The bishop is called by the stake president (a leader with spiritual stewardship over a regional area equivalent to a Catholic diocese), who is in turn called by regional authorities, and so on. From the stake president to the bishop, to the Sunday School teachers, everyone is a volunteer. In the case of time-intensive callings, such as the bishop, the Relief Society President (head of the women's organization), or Primary President (head of the children's organization), to be called is to be conscripted.

The assigned status of local leadership in Mormon communities means that pastoral duties like teaching doctrine, organizing activities, visiting the sick, and worrying about other people's rebellious teenagers are significant, and never far away. The bishop might be your neighbor, your gym partner, or your doctor. Hence, within Mormon congregations there is an unusual juxtaposition of familiarity and deference. When the bishop or the Relief Society President asks you to do something, you do it right away—not because you are a mindless drone, but because you know the weight of their burden.

When my father was called to be bishop of the Costa Mesa First Ward, he had to transition from being the goofy guy famous for loud snoring on church youth campouts and loud singing in the church choir to being the leader of the congregation. He was now responsible for the spiritual life of the ward, the economic welfare of needy families, and the representation of the church in the larger community.

Around the same time, my mother was called to be the Young Women's President, or the head of the organization for teenage girls. She changed her personality a bit to take on this new role, projecting more authority, more hipness, and expanding beyond her usual social circles. She called two other women to work with her as counselors. They met regularly in each others' homes to design lessons from "Choice and Accountability" to "Integrity" and to plan activities from volleyball to cake-decorating to wilderness survival. They knew each girl well and tried to ensure that lessons and activities were targeted to the girls' interests and needs.

From an early age I was also pressed into service, called to fill roles for which I was woefully underqualified. During my junior and senior year in high school, my piano teacher, Sister Barnes, who happened to be the ward organist, decided it was time for me to start playing the organ. She included hymns in my practice regimen, gave me a pair of organ shoes, and got me a key to the chapel. For the next two years, I held the members of the Costa Mesa First Ward hostage to my slow musical progress. When a hymn had difficult pedaling, I played it extra slow. When a hymn was easy, I sped through it. I ignored the exaggerated signals from the chorister, Sister Larsen, because I couldn't follow her lead and play the correct notes at the same time. Through it all, Sister Barnes sat with Brother Barnes in the pews, smiling.

To be Mormon is, in a sense, to be a professional amateur, always stretching and fitting yourself into the roles needing to be filled. Just as the chairs in the cultural hall are regularly reconfigured for different events, active Mormons regularly rearrange their lives to fulfill their duties, both welcome and dreaded, from vacuuming the carpet to preaching from the pulpit. This results in busy schedules and frequently bad sermons. It also creates community relationships that are multilayered and rich in history, in which the Sunday speaker both knows her audience and is known to them.

In the course of my life I've participated in Mormon communities all around the world for both short and long durations. I was a Young Women's teacher in Arlington, Massachusetts. I served in the Primary (children's organization) of my congregation in Hong Kong. I've entered a ward donut competition in Gyor, Hungary. I've painted squid with satay sauce for the ward Mid-Autumn Festival party in Tainan, Taiwan. I've rolled out the padded leather chairs in the corporate-boardroom-turned-Relief-Society-classroom in a Beijing corporate office tower. I've stacked up the tiny plastic chairs in the stone-walled garage that serves as the Primary room in Likasi, the Democratic Republic of the Congo. Even in places where I haven't spoken the language at all, I've always felt like I belonged. There are always chairs.

Chairs proved a bit problematic in Hong Kong when I served in the Primary of a small Mandarin-speaking congregation that met on the sixth floor of a high-rise church building in the bustling Wanchai district. There were only about seven children who came to Primary on Sunday, and frequently there were too many chairs. After five days under the stern authority of Hong Kong educators, the children who attended Primary came ready to let off steam. They used the chairs as footrests. They stacked them five high and sat on top. They even threw chairs at each other.

My own children attended the English-language Primary on the second floor, but because I spoke Mandarin, upon arriving in Hong Kong I volunteered to help the Primary President, Sister Dai. For nearly three years Sister Dai and I toiled together on Sunday mornings teaching lessons and songs. In a congregation composed mostly of mainland Chinese who had converted as adults, no one had grown up singing Primary songs or listening to Primary lessons. Hence, no one wanted to accept a Primary calling. Every Sunday it was Sister Dai and me alone against a band of pint-sized rebels.

There was a striking contrast between the Mandarin Primary, which met on the sixth floor, and the Primaries of the other church units meeting on different floors of the same building. In the Cantonese-speaking unit of local Hong Kongers on the fourth floor, for instance, the children were attentive and obliging. The difference was due not to "Chinese culture" but to a difference in critical mass and institutional maturity. The more children there were in Primary, the more it seemed like a proper learning institution with legitimate rules. The "institutionality" of Primary, therefore, itself became a source of strength.

This made me appreciate the magnitude of my cultural inheritance as a child raised in a mature Mormon congregation in Costa Mesa, California. Sturdy church institutional structures held together individuals, both children and adults, whose native impulse was to fly apart. Such community culture was the product of years and years of deliberate interaction in the chapel, the classroom, and the cultural hall.

I have never seen so many chairs in the cultural hall of the Costa Mesa ward building as on the day of my mother's funeral in December 2008. After enduring two years of physical pain and mental anguish caused by a rare cancer and the accompanying treatments, my mother passed away at home in the early morning. The two songs that she wanted performed at her funeral were both Primary songs: "I Feel

My Savior's Love," and "I'm Trying to Be Like Jesus." On the morning of the service, we opened up accordion partitions between the chapel and the gym to double the seating capacity and set out rows and rows of chairs. We unfolded dozens of Mom's beautiful quilts, the fruits of her recent years as a near-empty-nester, and hung them in tiers across the stage. The room was full of color and the chairs and side aisles were full of people.

My father, my mother's sister, my father's sister, my siblings and I all spoke. My cousins sang. Following the service, our family followed the hearse out to the cemetery overlooking the Pacific Ocean and said a final farewell. The sun was setting and the air was chilly.

We returned to the Costa Mesa building. Once again, the cultural hall had been transformed. The rows of chairs had vanished. Now there were five or six round tables, each covered with a white cloth and encircled by eight chairs. The hall was warm and bright and full of delicious smells. On the side near the kitchen, a dinner buffet of lasagna, rolls, and salad was waiting. Members of the Relief Society, like Sister Harmer and Sister Wills, had cooked the food, and now stood behind tables and served us with a quiet familiarity forged by decades of shared worship, planning, socializing, and service. That evening, as I leaned back in my chair, emotionally drained, warm, and relaxed, I felt how thoroughly we knew and were known. These had been my mother's people, and they were my people too.

Sometimes fellow Mormons become exhausted by being Mormon. Patriarchal administrative structures, in particular, have sapped many of my friends' enthusiasm. Another burden is history, the untidy and uncomfortably recent presence of Mormon leaders and members who, to put it mildly, said awkward things and made bad decisions.

And yet to me, Mormonism has never been primarily about church governance or church history. To me, Mormonism is a community built and held together by many hands. I believe with all my heart that some of these hands are divine, but I am also certain that most of them are human. I am often annoyed by patriarchal administrative structures, but my feelings shift considerably when I think about the "patriarchs" themselves: my husband, father, father-in-law, brothers, and beloved friends. I am often dismayed to feel the magnitude of mistakes made by leaders and members in church history, including racist policies and teachings. However, as I reflect on the participatory nature of church culture, I see that mistakes are inevitable just as growth is meaningful and ongoing.

I realize that the aspects of Mormonism that make me most uncomfortable are inextricably linked to those that I find most compelling. They are rooted in the kinship of flawed human beings, in the ties that bind us together in pain and glory.

I feel that life on earth is not a virtuoso operatic performance of angelic hosts, but a homely production in which a divine director is stuck with a troupe of second-string musicians and amateur actors who are always botching their lines. In the Mormon section of the orchestra pit, we stumble on, season after season: learning to play new instruments as needed, struggling to stay in tune, loyally attending rehearsal, folding and unfolding an endless array of chairs.

Just as in the story of Enoch and his city, the participatory nature of Mormon religiosity asserts that salvation is not an individual event, but a collective endeavor. Our building and rebuilding is not merely a means to an end. It is Zion itself.

NOTES

1. See Moses 6 & 7; The Pearl of Great Price. The scriptural canon for Mormons includes the Bible, the Book of Mormon, the Doctrine and Covenants, and the Pearl of Great Price.

Mourning with Those Who Mourn, Even when We Disagree with Them

by Michael Austin

MICHAEL AUSTIN received his BA and MA in English from Brigham Young University and his PhD in English Literature from the University of California at Santa Barbara. He is the author or editor of seven books and more than fifty articles, book chapters, and reviews. His most recent book, *Re-reading Job: Understanding the Ancient World's Greatest Poem*, is a sustained literary reading of the Book of Job from an LDS perspective. He is currently the Provost and Vice President of Academic Affairs at Newman University in Wichita, Kansas, where he lives with his wife, Karen, and his children, Porter and Clarissa.

"Why do the Members of Christ tear one another; why do we rise up against our own body in such madness; have we forgotten that we are all members, one of another?"–Pope St. Clement of Rome

From time to time, usually late at night after a day filled with frustrating encounters with other people, I try to imagine what might have happened in the American presidential election of 2012. What would have happened (I imagine) if Mitt Romney had won the presidency and Harry Reid had remained the Senate Majority Leader. Had such a thing occurred, the most powerful Republican and the most powerful Democrat in the United States would have been members of the Church of Jesus Christ of Latter-day Saints (Mormons). And because Mormons do not self-select into congregations, they might have ended up in the same ward. And this is where it gets good. With the Church's rotating lay leadership structure, either of them could have ended up becoming the other's bishop. One might have had to interview the other for worthiness to hold a temple recommend. They might have been home-teaching companions. And, at the very least, the two primary symbols of America's partisan dysfunction would have been obliged to worship together at least once a week and call each other "brother."

Regrettably, the world never got a chance to see Brothers Reid and Romney going to church together. But similar things happen on a smaller scale every week in LDS temples and meetinghouses around the world. In my own Wichita, Kansas ward, we have (including me) three fairly liberal college professor types, one Republican elected official, a number of well-informed moderates, several Tea Party conservatives, and about a hundred people who are too busy working and caring for their children to argue about politics. It is, in other words, a fairly typical LDS ward family, in which people who love and care for each other regularly come together and form meaningful spiritual bonds in spite of their different political persuasions, occupations, education levels, interests, social values, and respective understandings of their shared religion.

The same thing happens in most religious organizations, of course. But for Latter-day Saints, both the demands and the rewards of a diverse spiritual community are magnified by the enormous degree to which members of a ward become involved in each other's lives. Theologically, this involvement grows from the baptismal covenant articulated by the Book of Mormon prophet Alma when he baptized believers at the Waters of Mormon:

> And it came to pass that he said unto them: Behold, here are the waters of Mormon (for thus were they called) and now, as ye are desirous to come into the fold of God, and to be called his people, and are willing to bear one another's burdens, that they may be light;

> Yea, and are willing to mourn with those that mourn; yea, and comfort those that stand in need of comfort, and to stand as witnesses of God at all times and in all things, and in all places that ye may be in, even until death, that ye may be redeemed of God, and be numbered with those of the first resurrection, that ye may have eternal life.[1]

There aren't any loopholes here. Latter-day Saints are not called to determine who deserves to be mourned with, whose need for comfort meets the qualifications for comforting, or whose burdens really should be made light. We don't have to agree with the members of our ward family about much of anything. Profound disagreements about all sorts of issues are perfectly acceptable under the baptismal covenant in Mosiah. But we have made a covenant to love our fellow Saints anyway—to mourn with them, to comfort them, to bear their burdens, and to permit them to do the same for us. Another name for this covenant is "Zion."

Zion has always had something to do with reconciling conflicts, especially political ones. The Prophet Isaiah, whose writings are at the heart of the Latter-day Saint concept of Zion, prophesied of a time when Israel would be politically and spiritually united with both Egypt and Assyria—the two great warring superpowers of his day. "The Assyrians will link up with Egypt and the Egyptians with Assyria, and Egyptians will worship with Assyrians," he wrote. "When that day comes Israel will rank as a third with Egypt and Assyria and be a blessing in the world."[2] Such was the power of Isaiah's Zion that it could create people of one heart and one mind across the most daunting national and ideological boundaries in the world.

This idea of Zion has motivated Latter-day Saints from the very beginning. In 1829, before Joseph Smith founded the church, he received a revelation instructing him to "seek to bring forth and establish the cause of Zion."[3] Joseph taught his followers that, at least once in the history of the world, an entire city achieved such a high state of unity and righteousness that its inhabitants were taken directly to their celestial glory with their physical bodies still intact. This was the

City of Enoch—the patriarch (mentioned briefly in Genesis 5:21–24) whose city was called "Zion" because "they were of one heart and one mind, and dwelt in righteousness; and there was no poor among them."[4]

This version of Zion turned out to be a tough sell in nineteenth-century America. People of one heart and mind did not mix well with the rugged individualism of the American frontier. And large communities of people with a direct line to God rarely make good citizens of pluralistic societies—not least when God tells them to take more wives than law and custom allow. The biblical Zion was originally imagined in a society that was both theocratic and monarchical. It could not be transported to Jacksonian America without significant revisions. And try as they might, the Mormons have never been able to get away from the outside society whose pluralistic impulses allowed them to come into being in the first place.

So how does one go about building Zion in the middle of a pluralistic society? How can we accept our religious duty to be of one heart and one mind while at the same time fulfilling our civic responsibility to participate in an inherently adversarial political system? How do we become one with other people when we violently disagree with them on matters great and small? These are the dilemmas that Latter-day Saints face today when they seek to establish Zion. I can think of only three answers to this question: one of them is impossible, one of them is undesirable, and one of them is very hard.

The impossible answer is to make sure that everybody always thinks alike. But human nature just doesn't work like that. For inhabitants of the millennial world—the one where lions lie down with lambs—it might be possible to build a Zion where people see everything the same way. But it cannot happen in our world of fallen humans and fragmented perspectives. And if this is what we mean by "one heart and one mind," then we will just have to sit by the Waters of Babylon and weep—for, as Woody Allen reminds us, the lion and the lamb can lie down together in our world, but the lamb won't get much sleep.

The second option, the undesirable one, is to try to build Zion as an island of self-selected agreement in a sea of liberal pluralism. Too often, this has been the Saints' main Zion-creating strategy. Either they retreat to the mainly Mormon communities in the American West, where they can use the political process to set up the kind of society that makes them comfortable, or they set up socially self-sufficient wards and stakes in the midst of something that they often derisively term "the world." But this gets the whole concept wrong by conflating "Zion" with "the Church." This line of reasoning inevitably ends with a country-club version of Zion in which the Church sets up standards for correct belief and exiles those who fail to conform. The Church is not Zion, as Hugh Nibley reminds us, "the Church is a trial run for Zion, just as Zion is for paradise, and as paradise is for the heaven of God."[5]

This leaves the third option, which, while neither impossible nor undesirable, is really, really hard. We must find ways to disagree with each other about things that are very important to us while remaining people of one heart and one mind. This is hard because human beings are spectacularly bad at disagreeing without being disagreeable. Our evolutionary programming works against us. For one thing, our religious and our political beliefs come from the same cognitive places. They feel the same to us emotionally, so we have a hard time accepting that one group of beliefs can be morally essential in ways that others are not. Furthermore, when somebody disagrees with us, we feel personally attacked, and our fight-or-flight reflex kicks in. We have an overwhelming desire to run away or to lash out and label offending individuals as "them." But there can be no "thems" in the place we are trying to build. Everybody is "us" or it isn't Zion.

Building Zion is simply another name for becoming Zion people— a community of saints who have internalized the habits and attitudes that make Zion possible. These habits and attitudes include a willingness to see other human beings as part of the fabric that makes us possible. And it means treating everybody with the respect, love, and genuine commitment required for Zion to exist on the earth. When people like this get together in sufficient numbers, they cannot help but create Zion, which is simply the inevitable result of Zion people going about their business and interacting with each other according to their natures.

So, what does being a "Zion person" consist of? This is decidedly not a category in which I include myself, but it is something that has become a professional interest of mine. For the past two years, I have written a weekly opinion blog at the Internet Voter Network, a Web platform that emphasizes civil discussion and debate on important national and international issues. Many of my weekly posts are about the issues themselves, but just as many are about the ways that we discuss them. Over time, I have developed—in my mind and, hopefully, in my columns—a sort of aspirational type of the kind of person who can express opinions forcefully and still preserve relationships with all different kinds of people. I have written frequently about the characteristics of this type—characteristics that, I also believe, are important for those of us who want to build Zion in our fallen world. Among the most important characteristics of these prototypical "Zion people" are:

- **They understand that people disagree with each other because we all see the world through different filters and assumptions and not because they are crazy, stupid, or evil.** Most people are remarkably bad at this. Our own opinions seem so right to us that we cannot imagine another person not seeing things our way unless they are either misinformed or fundamentally flawed. In the abstract, we acknowledge that human diversity is a good thing, but with the concrete issues that we care about the most, we rarely see diversity as a strength.

- **They care more about human relationships than about winning arguments.** Most people don't mind being disagreed with, at least in theory, but we resent being belittled, insulted, and trivialized. Unfortunately, however, we are wired to perceive any challenge to our beliefs as a challenge to our legitimacy as human beings. The only way around this is to very clearly communicate respect when disagreeing with other people.

- **They try to understand actual points of disagreement.** Most people do most of their arguing with themselves, which is to say that we create a mental image of another person's position and spend our time responding to it rather than to what the other person is actually saying. But Zion requires mutual understanding. To be Zion people, we must interact with each other as fully formed children of God and not as shallow caricatures of human perspective. Here is a rule for disagreeing with people that, in my experience, never leads to the loss of a friend: *Never disagree with somebody's position until you can paraphrase that position back to the person who holds it in such a way that they say, "Yes, that is exactly what I meant."*

- **They recognize their own biases.** We all have them. We are all situated in a context, we all have interests, and we all have biases that affect how we structure arguments and admit evidence. We can't ever become unbiased (there is no not having a perspective), but we can try to recognize what our biases are and compensate for them when we are talking to other people whose biases may be very different.

- **They forgive.** Nobody ever gets these things right all the time. We are very attached to our opinions, and we often get carried away defending our beliefs. We will overreact. We will say things that we don't mean. We will take things personally. We will say things to hurt people. And people will do the same to us. Zion doesn't happen when we learn how to interact with each other perfectly; it happens when we learn how to forgive.

As I said, these are not easy habits to acquire. They go against the grain of human nature—not absolutely, the way trying to produce universal agreement does, but substantially and in ways we cannot ignore. Along with being carnal, sensual, and devilish, natural human beings are scared little mammals always on the lookout for potential threats to our wellbeing. Our reasoning skills largely evolved to win arguments, and our social cognition is better adapted to Machiavellian manipulation than to mutual respect. Like our closest cousins, the chimpanzees, we usually respond to people who challenge our beliefs and values with an almost irresistible impulse to start throwing poo.

But these are our demons. We are also children of God, and, as Abraham Lincoln observed in his First Inaugural Address, human nature has its "better angels" as well—characteristics that we all possess in some form and that can lead us much of the way to Zion. We derive pleasure from good relationships and are sustained by mutual trust and affection. We want to think well of people and be thought well of in return. We are programmed to try to understand other people's thoughts and emotions at the deepest levels. And we are capable genuine empathy—even when we disagree. The Kingdom of God really is within us if we are willing to look for it, and the great enterprise of building Zion is nothing less than the process of calling forth our better angels and making them a permanent part of our lives.[7]

NOTES

1. Mosiah 18: 8–9, Book of Mormon.

2. Isaiah 19:23–24, Revised English Bible.

3. Doctrine & Covenants 6:6.

4. Moses 7:18, Pearl of Great Price.

5. Hugh Nibley, *Approaching Zion* (Salt Lake City: Deseret Book and Provo: FARMS, 1989), 12.

6. I have adapted this list of traits of positive disagreement from my article "How to Argue with a Friend," first published on the Internet Voter Network web site on 12/11/13. See http://ivn.us/2013/12/11/argue-friend.

7. Steven Pinker discusses these "demons" and "good angels" of human nature at great length in *The Better Angels of Our Nature: Why Violence Has Declined* (New York: Penguin, 2011), 482–670.

Glimpses of Zion
By Patrick Q. Mason

PATRICK Q. MASON is the Howard W. Hunter Chair of Mormon Studies and Associate Professor of Religion at Claremont Graduate University. He is the author of *The Mormon Menace: Violence and Anti-Mormonism in the Postbellum South* and co-editor of *War and Peace in Our Time: Mormon Perspectives*.

Zion is the very heart of God's earthly vision for his family, and the great-unrealized project of Joseph Smith's restoration. Scholar Philip Barlow has recently written about the expansive, even breathtaking scope of Joseph's restoration vision. For Joseph, restoration was not just a matter of priesthood authority, true doctrine, and ecclesial structures—though no doubt each of those figured prominently. Joseph's restoration was about mending a fractured reality, about bringing healing and reconciliation to all the rifts, fissures, and chasms in creation—spiritual, political, economic, familial, cosmological, and so forth.[1]

This notion of restoration is evoked in modern theories and practices of restorative justice, which operates as a too-infrequently used alternative to our traditional models of retributive justice. Rather than focusing exclusively on the punishment and often removal from society of the perpetrator, restorative justice focuses on all stakeholders, including the perpetrator(s), victim(s), surrounding community, and government. Restorative justice embraces values such as encounter between victims, offenders, and affected community members; the expectation that offenders will make amends; and efforts to reintegrate and restore offenders as whole, productive members of the community. The focus is diverted from short-term removal of a lesion to long-term healing of the entire body, recognizing that the humanity of everyone involved, as well as the health of the social body, cannot be achieved simply via punishment.[2]

The relationship-centered ethos of reconciliation found in restorative justice is also the very basis of the Mormon version of Zion. The Zion-centered imagination belies the fallacy of individualistic salvation that owes more to the modern Enlightenment notions of personal autonomy and fulfillment than to the more community-oriented teachings of millennia of prophets, from ancient Hebrews to modern Mormons. Zion is a collective striving for the "beloved community" spoken of by Martin Luther King, Jr. In Zion we are saved together or not at all. Zion breaks down artificially constructed boundaries of tribe and time by holding that all of God's family, living and dead, is caught in a web of inextricable mutuality, that "they without us cannot be made perfect—neither can we without our dead be made perfect."[3]

And so it is only natural that in Zion there is no presence of "any manner of -ites," for in Zion we are all "in one, the children of Christ."[4] The disparate nations of the earth, predicated upon and propagating as they do the very notion of "[all] manner of -ites," are the betrayal of the family of God. Zion is the restoration of the fractured reality of Babel as depicted in the biblical story. Zion tears down the great and spacious buildings that set themselves up as replacements for God, and enthrones God at the center of a community that reverses the tragedy of division of the families of the earth. Zion restores a human community before nationalism, before class division, even before fratricidal violence, the first of humanity's social sins.

In my life and church experience I have enjoyed two glimpses of Zion—one in South Bend, Indiana, the other in Cairo, Egypt. No one would confuse either locale with Paradise: the former is a typical mid-sized Midwestern Rust Belt city decades past its prime, the other a barely functioning, overcrowded, and polluted megalopolis centuries (millennia?) beyond its heyday. But in both places my wife and I found a deeply meaningful community of care in the local Mormon ward or branch. All the markers of human division—race, class, gender, profession, status—mattered less than one's presence and willingness to serve. "We're just glad you're here" was the prevailing ethos. Nobody cared so much what crazy ideas you had, so long as you showed up, and especially so long as you were willing to extend yourself on behalf of others. In South Bend that typically meant ministry in the economically depressed and predominantly non-white western half of the city. In Cairo it meant forming an alternative extended family for people of a wide range of nationalities, virtually all of whom were thousands of miles away from "home." In both cases the church became a laboratory for transcending the fractures that typically divide us, and brought the members together in common cause and sentiment.

To be clear, neither South Bend nor Cairo was Zion. Far from it. Both failed—and in this they have plenty of company—in effectively addressing, let alone overturning, structural inequalities based on race, gender, wealth, and nationality. Both failed to live up to the standard of having no contention, envy, or strife.[5] Both were surrounded by multigenerational poverty but failed to make a dent. But in both of these graced communities I often had glimpses of Zion, all-too-ephemeral tastes of what it might look like to come together "in one, the children of Christ," without regard to "any manner of –ites." Both gave me concrete hope that fracture and fissure are not the destiny of human society, certainly not of the body of Christ.

Part of the Mormon Zion is redemptively forced upon us by the fact that we do not choose our congregation. Mormonism may be the last holdout of the parish system of medieval Catholicism, where your religious community was defined by your geographic community, not by personal preference. Choice enters into it because of natural socioeconomic divisions, but especially in places outside the Mormon Culture Region, the limited number of church members means that wards are geographically large and typically take in a range of different neighborhoods, thus throwing together people who would not otherwise associate with each other in virtually any civic capacity. Although lingering effects of historic race-based policies have limited Mormonism's appeal to African Americans, in urban areas Mormon wards are remarkably integrated, and no one bats an eye.

Mormonism is still catching up on racial diversity, but there is no doubt that it encompasses significant socioeconomic diversity. It is not uncommon for a ward to have millionaires and food stamp recipients serving together in a Relief Society or Young Men's presidency—where else does that happen? The ideal classlessness of Mormon community was brought home to me by a comment made by a recent convert to the church in South Bend named Kelly. He was a janitor at Notre Dame, where several of us were professors or graduate students. On that campus, as at most campuses and other places of work, janitors are practically invisible, and occupy a distinctly lower place in the de facto caste system. But Kelly and his wife Kathy were amazing people, and immediately endeared themselves to the ward. They became part of the dinner circuit, and Kelly and I served together in a number of capacities, sharing lots of laughs in the process. When my mother came to visit and met Kelly, he hugged her and said, "Isn't this a great church, where a janitor and a professor at Notre Dame can be friends?" In a nutshell, that's what it means to have "no manner of –ites."

I think that Latter-day Saints have sometimes suffered somewhat from a lack of definitional clarity as they have thought and talked about Zion. At times we have conflated Zion and the church, as if they are one and the same—or at least that the former is an idealized, perfected version of the latter. This confusion is understandable, and a number of scriptures could be cited which seem to point in that direction. But a careful reading of an important March 1831 revelation to Joseph Smith offers a more capacious view.

This 1831 revelation includes apocalyptic language regarding the end-times prior to Jesus Christ's Second Coming, during which the earth would be in tumult, both from natural disasters as well as from the violence of God's children who "harden their hearts" and "take up the sword, one against another, and . . . kill one another," resulting in "wars in foreign lands" and "wars in your own lands." God's people, however, were not to participate in this worldly violence. The revelation commanded the "elders of the church" to gather as many people as would heed their call to Zion, "the New Jerusalem, a land of peace, a city of refuge, a place of safety for the saints of the Most High God." Zion here is envisioned not simply or even primarily as a harbor from spiritual tempests. Rather, it constitutes in a very real sense a refuge from violence—for the early Mormon Saints, yes, but also for "every man that will not take his sword against his neighbor." In short, Zion would be a cosmopolitan community of peace: "And there shall be gathered unto it out of every nation under heaven; and it shall be the only people that shall not be at war one with another."[6] We see something of this spirit of inclusiveness in the original composition of the Council of Fifty—imagined by Joseph Smith in his final years to be an integral part of the government of the millennial kingdom of God—which included three non-Latter-day Saints as full voting members.[7] In sum, the gathered church is in Zion, but Zion is not simply and exclusively the gathered church—any more than the church has a monopoly on "the pure in heart."[8]

If Zion is a restoration of God's family, then somewhat ironically it can only be accomplished by speaking prophetically toward much of what has come to be accepted as the modern family, particularly in the United States. Here I am speaking not of the increasing pluralism of the types of relationships that are legally and culturally constituted as families, and which many Latter-day Saints have spent so much time and energy wringing their hands over (not to mention politically mobilizing against). To be sure, we can and should talk about whether non-heterosexual, non-monogamous relationships fundamentally undermine (or advance) the Zion project. But alongside those debates which have too often been a source of discord and division rather than reconciliation and restoration—we must consider the place of the "traditional" nuclear family in Zion.

In Zion people are "married, and given in marriage."[9] At the same time, Zion resists the idolatry of the family. The absence of "–ites" in the Book of Mormon Zion is a deliberate and direct critique of the modus operandi of most of the history of the Lehites and Jaredites, namely that people who were originally all from the same family eventually divided into tribes ("–ites") and then spent a considerable amount of their time, talent, and treasure demonizing and then killing the other branch of the family. This is only possible when the family becomes an idol—an object of adoration and a barrier between humans and the worship of the true God. The Book of Mormon and Old Testament both excel at revealing how the family (and its mythic extension, the nation) too easily becomes an image and model of social organization predicated on boundary-drawing exclusion rather than boundary-disrupting inclusion. The nuclear family is at its best a microcosm of Zion, a means to an end, not an end in itself. Jesus warned his disciples repeatedly that they would have to be willing to forsake the nuclear family for the cause of Zion—a troubling requirement that does not often make it onto lists of his most popular teachings.[10]

So the residents of Zion learn to affirm and live in families without idolizing them. Zion strives to find the precarious balance between care for the particular and care for the whole. The astonishingly ambitious program of seeking to seal together all the descendants of Eve and Adam is not an attempt to celestialize a model of 1950s middle-class American domesticity, but rather to restore to wholeness the entirety of the human family. Our sacred sealing rituals are meant to weld together all of God's children and point us toward the universality of the family of God, not to instrumentalize the particularity of tribe and clan. Zion is not a suburb; Joseph Smith's "Plat of the City of Zion" was not a prophetic anticipation of Levittown.

We do not live in Zion; we can hardly even see it from here. But occasionally we catch glimpses, whether through scriptural passages that are tantalizing in their brevity or in lived experiences that leave us with the feeling that we are, in that fleeting moment, coming close. Zion is individual, though it cannot be achieved with personal conversion. It is structural, though it cannot be accomplished with a government or church program. It is cultural, though it cannot be actualized through telling the right stories and singing the right songs. Zion may seem the very embodiment of the Sisyphean task. But if it occupies our minds and hearts, becoming the frame of our individual and collective moral imaginations, then we may find ourselves closer to it than we ever thought possible. And in that Zionic time and place we begin to discover the true meaning of restoration.

NOTES

1. See Philip L. Barlow, "To Mend a Fractured Reality: Joseph Smith's Project," *Journal of Mormon History* 38:3 (Summer 2012): 28–50.

2. See http://www.restorativejustice.org/university-classroom/01introduction (accessed June 9, 2014).

3. Doctrine & Covenants 128:15.

4. 4 Nephi 1:17, Book of Mormon.

5. See 4 Nephi 1:3, 15–16, Book of Mormon.

6. Doctrine & Covenants 45:33, 63, 66, 69.

7. An 1882 revelation to church president John Taylor said of the original composition of the Council of Fifty, "I [the Lord] moved upon [Joseph Smith] to introduce into my Kingdom certain parties not in my Church." Quoted in Andrew F. Ehat, "'It Seemed Like Heaven Began on Earth': Joseph Smith and the Constitution of the Kingdom of God," *BYU Studies* 20:3 (Spring 1980): 257.

8. Doctrine & Covenants 97:21.

9. 4 Nephi 1:11, Book of Mormon. Many readers will be quick to point out that the verse does not explicitly say how those marriages were constituted, merely that marriage was a cornerstone of the society.

10. See Mark 10:29–30; Luke 9:59–62.

As Sisters in Zion
By Julie M. Smith

JULIE M. SMITH graduated from the University of Texas at Austin with a BA in English and added an MA in Biblical Studies from the Graduate Theological Union in Berkeley, CA. She is on the executive board of the Mormon Theology Seminar, is a contributing writer at Times & Seasons, and is the author of *Search, Ponder, and Pray: A Guide to the Gospels* and a forthcoming commentary on the Gospel of Mark.

Does Mormonism oppress women—or liberate them? This question has been posed in virtually every phase of the church's history: in the nineteenth century (when the oppressing and/or liberating agent was polygamy), in the twentieth century (when it was full-time homemaking for super-sized families) and today (when the focus is on the male-only priesthood). The project of Zion-building has always been tethered to tensions regarding the role of women in Zion: would they be polygamous wives and/or happy homemakers and/or priestesses?

Complicated by broader cultural fluctuations as well as by internal divisions, the answers have never been obvious. It may seem absurd to suggest something like polygamy could ever liberate women, but some Mormon women have made that argument, noting that polygamy made it possible for some women to pursue advanced degrees while their "sister wives" raised their children and the demographic imbalance it created gave women (who were permitted to divorce; men generally were not) quite a bit of leverage in the marriage market. I must admit that it would have been tempting to hand off the full-time mothering of toddlers—something to which I was not temperamentally suited in the least—to another person, even if I had to share my husband with her. Of course, others conclude that polygamy devalued women and left them with little financial or emotional support. These interpretive fault lines have wended their way throughout Mormon history and into the present time. Today, Mormon women can generally be divided into three main groups in terms of their approaches to women's issues in the church. Interestingly enough, each group maps onto a woman's story from the Book of Mormon—and given that there are barely three such stories, that's a rather neat feat.

I. SARIAH

In the opening pages of the Book of Mormon, Sariah's family flees into the wilderness to escape the coming destruction of Jerusalem—a destruction known only through the visions of her husband. But realizing that they have no access to their sacred scriptures, they send their sons back into the fray to retrieve the record. Sariah mourns what she presumes to be the death of her sons and complains about her husband, Lehi. He attempts to comfort her but is unsuccessful. It is not until the sons return safe and in possession of the record that Sariah can proclaim that she knows "of a surety" that her husband's visions were genuine.

What I see in Sariah's story is a woman with a bone-deep fidelity to the male visionary who is her religious leader. After all, she did leave everything she owned to follow him into the desert. At the same time, her personal alienation from divine communication leaves her mourning and unable to be consoled by the comfort that her male leader offers, despite his best efforts. It is only through her own personal experience that she is able to obtain peace. I see Sariah in today's moderate Mormon feminists: they prioritize their commitment to the church, but they mourn the lack of opportunities for women to independently engage the divine and to experience leadership opportunities. For example, priesthood blessings are given for comfort, counsel, and healing—but only by male priesthood holders. Some women, including myself, have mourned the inability to turn to a trusted female friend for a blessing in situations where it would be uncomfortable to discuss the need for the blessing with a man. These moderate feminists see Zion-building as involving a delicate balance between advocating for some changes while maintaining loyalty to the institutional church. They do have a lot to be grateful for in the last decade or so of Mormon history, as some modifications have given Mormon women greater voice and visibility without undermining the basic structure of the church. These changes have included permitting women to pray at the church's general conferences, lowering the age at which women can serve as missionaries (which means that far more are serving), and creating leadership opportunities for these female missionaries.

II. ABISH

Later in the Book of Mormon,[1] super-missionary Ammon converts a king, who falls to the ground. Many in his court believe him to be dead; his own wife is uncertain. When she—along with the rest of his court—also fall as if dead, chaos erupts. Abish, a servant and secret convert, is the only one left standing; she runs from house to house to explain that, contrary to the conclusion that others are reaching, Ammon has not brought evil upon them; rather, he is a man of God.

In Abish's narrative, I see the more conservative women of Mormonism. They realize things look bad to the larger world: a church banning women from all significant leadership roles and from the performance of religious ordinances will garner no plaudits in the modern world. But for these women, the problem is not the practice but the perception, so they run from house to house to explain that things are not what they appear. The church is not bringing evil into women's lives any more than Ammon brought it into the king's court:

Mormonism, in their view, liberates women by exalting motherhood and women's natural instincts to nurture. The importance that motherhood is granted in Mormon rhetoric made it marginally easier for me to endure baby-filled days and sleepless nights—there was never any doubt that my religious leaders believed that the work that I was doing was essential. By positioning the work that women have traditionally performed as worthy of the highest praise, Mormonism validates and rewards what is essentially female. These conservative women see Zion-building as resisting the pressure to mold the church to fit new beliefs about gender. They view the emphasis in LDS discourse on female modesty, homemaking, and an all-male priesthood as important recognition of women's unique roles.

III. MORIANTON'S MAID

In a brief and rarely-noted narrative hidden in the dense "war chapters" of the Book of Mormon, a female servant of the enemy leader Morianton escapes from his camp after he viciously beats her.[2] She reveals his military plans to the good guys, who are able to intervene to prevent his intentions from coming to fruition. In this narrative, the most liberal Mormon feminists see their story: they must escape at least some of their previous beliefs and practices and reveal the oppression in the system, perhaps to outsiders, so that it will not be permitted to continue. They view the ban on women's priesthood ordination on par with the church's previous ban on the ordination of men of African descent: a practice stemming from a prejudiced culture that then accumulated traditions and justifications to support it, but which must be rooted out in order for Zion to flourish. They see some recent changes in the church, such as the reversal of the policy banning the broadcast of the all-male general priesthood meetings, as a result of their efforts to publicize the church's exclusion of women from priesthood and leadership roles. While I do not personally desire to expose Mormonism's gender-related practices to the scorn of the outside world, I do understand the desire to see change by any vector possible. I do feel a sense of mission to uncover the "hidden gems" of equality from scripture and church history. I take every opportunity I can find—through writing, blogging, and teaching—to bring out of obscurity the stories of women's past leadership and witness. Little makes me happier than watching the faces of a class as they learn that, in addition to the men they have been hearing about for their entire lives, there was also a female witness to the Book of Mormon.

Of course, grouping all Mormon women into three divisions is horribly reductionist. This schema doesn't even work for just me: depending on the day, you might find me in any one of the three camps or, more likely, trying to straddle two—if not all three!—of them. This kind of tension, and the cognitive dissonance it produces, is a major source of stress for some Mormon women.

And yet this tripartite outline does at least provide a sense that not only are women's issues a major concern in Mormonism, but there are a variety of schools of thought on the issues. This has always been the case.

But what is new today is the way in which the online world impacts women's issues in real-world Mormonism. From mommy blogs to Pinterest to the "Bloggernacle"—a name derived from the beloved Mormon Tabernacle Choir and applied to the major Mormon blogs—to countless Facebook discussions, the current iteration of angst over the roles of Mormon women is playing out in an unprecedented way: for the first time, each and every Mormon woman who wants a platform for her views can find one. Mormon women are using those platforms not only to expound on women's issues but also on how Mormonism impacts their lives, in what has become a grassroots example of online Zion-building, where any woman whose writings strike a chord may end up influencing a worldwide audience. Zion will never be the same.

Women in each group see themselves as building up Zion by advocating for their distinct approach to gender issues: from the reproduction of quotations from church leaders on Pinterest, to advocacy-oriented Facebook groups, to essays hosted by a multitude of personal and Bloggernacle blogs. The institutional church has also responded to the new media landscape with a far more active public affairs department—which, perhaps not coincidentally, now has spokes*women*—whose statements regularly send waves of frenetic discussion through online LDS groups; Mormon missionaries, of which an increasingly large percentage are women, are also increasingly an online presence.

None of this is to suggest that all is well in Zion. The recent excommunication of Mormon feminist Kate Kelly—a woman who leveraged social and traditional media to advance her cause of the ordination of LDS women—sent panic through liberal and some moderate LDS feminists as they worried that any expression of divergence from current church doctrine or practice might be met with church discipline. The church—first, through its public affairs office and then through a statement from its highest leaders—clarified that the line would be drawn not at raising questions but at advocacy: inquirers would not be punished, but organizers might be. What is most remarkable about these events is not that they occurred (this is not the first time an advocate of Mormon feminism has been disciplined by the church) but the speed at which they played out—and the fact that Mormons all over the world (the ones who were interested, anyway) not only witnessed them in real time but could comment in their preferred online venue.

And comment they did. Kate Kelly's excommunication was widely lamented and caused deep wounds within the Mormon community, partially because pundits on all sides behaved more like partisans than like saints: harsh comments, invitations to leave the church, and comparisons to history's very worst moments litter online discussions of LDS women's issues. These voices violate not only the Mormon norm of niceness but also the larger Christian call to kindness. Reading through some of these discussions has left me wondering if online discussions might extinguish any hope of Zion. There is no doubt that women on both sides have been wounded during these discussions. On the other hand, women who have felt isolated in their local Mormon congregations for their liberal beliefs can now engage the like-minded online; this validation may help them to remain within the fold. Similarly, more conservative women can enjoy a celebration of creative homemaking as an aspirational lifestyle on numerous blogs and on Pinterest.

The phrase "as sisters in Zion" is well-known to LDS women, who sing a hymn by that name which, in its antiquated cadences, announces that "we'll all pull together" to "build up the kingdom with earnest endeavor." There is no doubt that Mormon women are employing tools both old and new to build up Zion even if their visions of that kingdom are not always entirely compatible.

NOTES

1. See Alma 19, Book of Mormon.

2. See Alma 50, Book of Mormon.

On "Enid vs. The Big Tent"
by Scott Hales

SCOTT HALES is a cartoonist and college English professor in the Cincinnati area. He has a PhD in English from the University of Cincinnati and specializes in American literature and Mormon fiction. His comics and writing have appeared in various publications, including *Sunstone, Dialogue: A Journal of Mormon Thought and Religion and the Arts*. His webcomic *The Garden of Enid: Adventures of a Weird Mormon Girl* (www.thegardenofenid. tumblr.com) received a special award in comics from the Association for Mormon Letters in 2014. He blogs about Mormon literature at www.artisticpreaching.wordpress.com.

One of the challenges of establishing Zion today is adapting a nineteenth-century vision to the realities of twenty-first century life. In "Enid vs. The Big Tent," a Mormon teenager struggles to find a metaphor that adequately resolves the tension between inclusion and exclusion, which is always a problem at the heart of communal ideals. Scripture dictates, after all, that the righteous flee to Zion as a refuge from the wickedness and violence of the world.[1] In everyday life, drawing such a line in the sand and ensuring that everyone gets (and stays) on the right side is always easier said than done. In the nineteenth century, Mormons tried to build an actual City of Zion in Jackson County, Missouri, with disastrous results. Their disappointment in this endeavor forced them—and their successors—to reevaluate the form Zion should take. While they have done this more or less

"OPEN RANGE MORMONISM" might work better...
... but I think that one fails too... in mistaking all BORDERS for WALLS.
Because... I mean... we're asked to "ENLARGE [our] BORDERS"*... because BORDERS HELP us DEFINE who we ARE in more ways than we probably REALIZE...
MORE GOOD
So... maybe we could use an umbrella metaphor...
...since umbrellas create a "BORDER" between us and RAIN...
... without limiting our VIEW... or closing us off entirely.
If only they were BIGGER...
*Moroni 10:31

Joseph Smith imagined the Church as a CITY laid out in an orderly GRID...
CITY LIMIT
ZION
... that would EXPAND its BOUNDARIES as it welcomed more PEOPLE in...
In this CITY... people would live in HARMONY, but tend to individual STEWARDSHIPS tailored to personal NEEDS and STRENGTHS...
...and CELESTIAL LAW... not CULTURAL TRADITION... would guide the AFFAIRS of the PEOPLE... ensuring JUSTICE and MERCY...
So... maybe instead of "BIG TENT MORMONISM" we could say "EXPANDING GRID MORMONISM"... or IDK ... use the WORD the LORD used: "ZION"...
MORE GOOD

successfully, the challenge of giving shape to Zion remains unfulfilled, largely because people continue to be imperfect and human. Personal righteousness—that pursuit of moral and ethical being—is a process taking the individual on a journey down some complicated paths. The question for Zion's gatekeepers—whoever they are—is whether Zion should be a space for these paths or the reward at the end of the journey.

In the comic, I try to make a case for a Zion that opens its gates for these often unpredictable paths. Enid begins with a critique of the term "Big Tent Mormonism," which has lately come to signify the most liberal vision of contemporary Zion: a Church that invites all to come unto Christ and shelters them in the refining process of His atonement, no matter the idiosyncrasies their journeys might exhibit. While Enid agrees with the sentiment, she struggles with a metaphor that ultimately throws up impermeable walls between people, as a big tent does. Likewise, she resists metaphors that do away with boundaries altogether or that suggest too little space. For her, Zion should be a kind of amorphous space that gathers people within borders that aren't fixed and impermeable.

To find this space, Enid returns to Joseph Smith's original plan for the City of Zion, which he and his advisors drew up in the early 1830s to give order to the Latter-day Saints' initially haphazard efforts at Zion-building in western Missouri. While not without its flaws and oversights—critics have noted, for instance, that the square mile the plan allotted for Zion would be cramped for its proposed 15,000 to 20,000 inhabitants—Smith's holy city was to be a space in which people and nature lived harmoniously around a center where politics, commerce, industry, and education were sanctified by the presence of sacred temples. More importantly, though, the plan allowed for expansion and growth. If the population got too big in Zion, it could expand by replicating itself on adjacent lands—ideally until all the world was incorporated into its city limits. The borders of Zion, therefore, were to be fluid and permeable as well as distinct and secure from the rest of the world. For Enid, this kind of porous, elastic border speaks more to her sense of Zion than the border implied by the big tent.

Interestingly, Joseph Smith's plan for the City of Zion was not originally part of my plan for "Enid vs. The Big Tent." At first, I'd planned to draw up a three-page comic with Enid endorsing an umbrella metaphor for the Mormon Church because of the way it does away with walls while retaining something of a protective border. As I drew and thought more about the umbrella, I became dissatisfied with the metaphor. If nothing else, the big tent has size going for it, even if that size is eventually restricted by a heavy canvas wall. The umbrella solves the wall problem, but takes a giant step backwards in terms of size. Sure, I told myself, there are some really big umbrellas out there, but not big enough for the kind of metaphor I had in mind. I needed something more ambitious for Enid—something I felt she could buy into without reservation.

That's when I remembered the City of Zion. For the past decade or so, I have been fascinated by Joseph Smith's dream of building a sacred city—a dream he shared with many utopians of his day. As a teenager, I'd traveled to Independence, Missouri, where Smith had planned to build Zion, and stood on the spot where he and his followers had laid cornerstones for a temple. Mormons have never given up hope that the site there will be reclaimed for Zion, and currently several churches in the Latter-day Saint tradition act as caretakers of the spot. I knew this and felt a deep reverence for the destiny of that space. Later, after studying the plan more, I discovered that the original plan for Zion, because of its logistical oversights, perhaps works better as a metaphor than a practical piece of urban planning. It calls on believers to organize their lives around a government that harmonizes the spiritual, intellectual, and physical needs of a united people. It beautifies the land through orderly architecture and gardens, suggesting cooperation with nature rather than its exploitation. And it opens its boundaries to all who choose to live a more enlightened way of being. The city, in other words, offers an ideal vision not only for all of our interactions and relationships, but also for the systems and constructs we use to order and organize them. Zion is a blueprint for marriages, families, friendships, communities, congregations, clubs, and nations. Zion maps our greatest priorities and gives us direction.

Like all large communities, the LDS Church has divisions that compete for the minds and hearts of believers. Latter-day scripture, however, defines Zion as a righteous people who are "of one heart and one mind." This does not mean Zion's aim is to diminish the agency and individuality of its inhabitants. Rather, Zion encourages us to consecrate, or devote, our agency and individuality to the betterment of all. For me, Zion needs a border that is easily crossed and navigated to ensure that this betterment is open to all who want and need it.

In the second to last panel of "Enid vs. The Big Tent," I depict an urban Zion with a homey, tree-lined neighborhood with a distant skyline of high-rise buildings behind it. I doubt this is what Zion will look like, but my goal was to convey the harmony between apparent opposites that seems central to the early prophet's Zion plan. What Zion does is give us hope we can reconcile the many conflicts and divisions keeping us separate and apart. If the rural can harmonize with the urban, if the spiritual can harmonize with the intellectual or political, why can't we harmonize with each other?

In the foreground of this panel are two people. Originally, I had drawn two throwaway characters to represent the happy inhabitants of Zion. As I was finishing the panel, though, my seven-year-old daughter said I should put us in the panel instead. I liked the idea—not because I think my home has achieved anything close to a Zion-like state, but because Zion is the kind of place I would like for my family. We try our best to work together and do our part to establish Zion in our home and community, and I'd like to think we make a small difference. Fortunately, Zion is an ongoing process of communal refinement. As we strive to better ourselves within its borders, we break down the walls of our hearts and open them to those who wish to share in our joy.

NOTES

1. See Doctrine and Covenants 45.65–69.

By Their Fruit (Lands) Ye Shall Know Them
by Tona Hangen

TONA HANGEN is an associate professor at Worcester State University, where she teaches courses in American history. She writes about religion and broadcast media, blogs about history pedagogy, and writes as a contributing editor at The Juvenile Instructor. She and her husband are the parents of four children and they live on a small farm in central Massachusetts.

"Thus these modern pilgrims journeyed hopefully out of the old world, to found a new one in the wilderness."

–LOUISA MAY ALCOTT, "TRANSCENDENTAL WILD OATS," 1873

I live in Zion. My faith in this fact is annually renewed on autumn days when the sun slants through acres of gilded maple trees as if through sky-high stained glass windows, when crimson leaves cavort across my path and the hills blaze with celestial fire like Moses's bush, and at such moments no one can convince me otherwise. And, as it turns out, I am not alone. Many have thought so before me. Algonquin tribes believed that our earth (of which, naturally, New England was the center) was a land resting on the back of a turtle. And that turtle rested on another turtle. And below that? It was turtles all the way down. Likewise, scratch the historical surface of the land lying within my ward and stake boundaries and you will find messy layers of former Zions. We are Zion all the way down.

My Mormon ward encompasses twelve bucolic New England towns, redolent with apple trees, pumpkin fields, slow-moving rivers, hardwood forests, spring-fed ponds, and stony cobbled soil, each one pinned to the map by a white Congregational church steeple on the surviving town green. By all appearances, we look the very model of the seedbed of American character: democratic self-government, individualistic striving, tirelessly reshaping the landscape in the service of economic development with brick mills, canals, railroads, and stone walls running through (now) dense woodlands as evidence of our ancestors' zeal for clearing and profit-making. But this same land also cultivated an equally American counterculture: fire-breathing revival, prophetic preaching, radical reform, and unconventional religious imagination.

Littleton, the town which lends its name to the ward, was founded as one of a dozen seventeenth-century Puritan missionary communities for so-called praying Indians—converts to Christianity for whom the first Bible translation in America was printed. A plaque, now in the middle of a peach orchard, describes how Littleton's praying Indians' loyalty was questioned during King Philip's War, hence their removal to Deer Island in Boston Harbor where most of them died of disease and starvation. Indian names are a tattered remnant, flowing like faint music across our landscape: Narragansett, Wachusett, Pompositicut, Nobscot, Nashua. Across these fields and town commons minutemen mustered to fight the early battles of the Revolutionary War; in these towns their wives wove homespun to flaunt their economic independence.

In the 1780s, the charismatic, visionary founder of the Shakers, Mother Ann Lee, saw this place in a dream before coming to found her headquarters (the "Eastern Bishopric") and establish some of the earliest Shaker towns in Harvard and Shirley. In the 1840s during the era of manifestations, the Harvard Shakers built a fenced hilltop bower they called the Holy Hill of Zion. It still survives, reached from a short steep trail off a housing tract street; a cemetery of neatly marked Shaker graves in the woods attests to their longevity and sense of gendered order.

Early in the nineteenth century, Baptists—then radical religious upstarts prohibited from having their own place of worship—built a stone altar atop what is now the local ski hill. Transcendentalist and vegetarian zealot Bronson Alcott removed his family and a handful of fellow reform enthusiasts here in 1843 for a short-lived "consociate family" experiment he called Fruitlands. Just over the ward boundary in genteel Concord lies Walden Pond, "earth's eye . . . into which the beholder measures the depth of his own nature," where Thoreau launched his own experiment in radical simplicity and communicating with the divine through the turn of nature's seasons. In those same years of the early 1840s followers of the energetic Adventist William Miller congregated throughout central Massachusetts; in Groton and Lancaster (also within our ward boundaries) believers waited for the Second Coming one cold October night that became the "Great Disappointment."

The neighborhood of my ward, then, is the cradle of American utopias, where fervent dreamers have planted the hope of Zion season after season, including during the era of Mormonism's founding. I find this both deeply ironic and strangely hopeful: a people's collective longing to be a holy commonwealth and collapse the distance between the mundane and the divine—this has been tried here before, on the same grounds, under the same autumn-blazing trees, beside the same lakes, accompanied by the same birdsong. Each of these former Zions drew its elements from a common well: charismatic leaders, radical rejection of capitalist and hidebound religion's values, reinventing the prevailing social and economic order in favor of communal social organization, unshakeable sense of holy mission, commitment to self-purification and sacrifice for a greater good. In an odd way, and surely without acknowledging the debt, twenty-first century Mormons carry on the American legacy of Zion-building in one place where this impulse was first fanned to a flame.

My ward began as a branch organized for military families stationed at Fort Devens in 1957, the year of Sputnik. Until 1968 the branch met on base, then in various local community buildings, until in 1978 it split into two wards and the church acquired a potato field ("Sheridan Acres") for a chapel of its own, dedicated in 1981. For years ward members cultivated apples and vegetables on nearby land as a welfare farm, unconsciously replicating the Fruitlands experiment, farming by hand as a consociate community. Fort Devens is now closed, replaced by a National Guard facility, maximum security prison, and high-tech community redevelopment. Like everywhere in America, our towns' demographics are changing. The ward missionaries now live in an apartment complex alongside recently arrived software engineers from India and West Africa; we translate stake conference meetings into Spanish, Portuguese, and Cambodian.

Of course our modern Zion-dwellers do not farm fields and orchards full-time, nor hew their own homes out of the dense woods. Today, most make their living in the American post-industrial service economy. Here, the Church functions as a massive, corporatized bureaucracy, centrally organized and peripherally administered, churning out ceaseless rounds of meetings, programs, correlated curricula, duties and responsibilities, and handbooks. Wards like mine are, in one sense, mere periphery to Salt Lake's center—but in another sense, they are the church's living, beating heart.

When my husband and I moved into the ward, I was a graduate student and young mother of two small boys, a transplant from Virginia who had come to New England for college and never left. We traded a home on a noisy city block for a farmhouse and barn in need of some repair, and began growing chickens, farm animals, flowers, and food. We have dug in deeply, blending our two careers—a surgeon and a college professor—while raising four socially conscious and kind children. My lived experience over nearly twenty years in my Zion ward overflows with rich, complicated human relationships irreducible to any handbook or program. People have loved me and my family fiercely, completely, protectively, but without judgment. I have felt utterly accepted for who I am, even while being challenged and mentored to be better. I've stood at hospital bedsides, served funeral luncheons, showered new babies, packed and unpacked moving vans, given rides, cooked meals, applauded talent shows, stayed late to clean up, and often unburdened myself on others' sturdy shoulders. I've given away the best of myself to the one who might appear least deserving, partly because I've been such a regular recipient of that same grace and mercy. Young people I knew as teens grew up, went away on missions or to college, got married, moved back home, had children of their own. I've seen the ward's arms open to the homeless, the tattooed, the misfit, the terminally ill, the cynical, and the hurting alike. Such gifts of human kindness are the warp and woof of a modern Zion; they transcend the very real challenges posed by economic uncertainty, identity politics, the information tsunami, and our frenetic pace of life. They strengthen a connecting thread with our "old" Zions—whose people imagined a nourishing alternative to whatever was most soul-numbing in their own time, and labored tirelessly to build a holy city open to all who would like to live in that reimagined world. My Zion ward offers a respite from relentless, slickly polished but empty commercialism, from technology-driven social isolation, and from measuring one's achievement by earning power alone. It's messy and difficult, but sweet is the work.

Does my Zion (and all the Zions planted here before it) hold any lessons for twenty-first-century Mormonism as a whole? If they do, it might be this: we achieve Zion by embracing the one. Not "the one" as some mystical unity of all believers, but one person at a time. Zion can be envisioned globally, but it must be grown locally and at human scale. We cultivate Zion by consciously choosing to love someone other than ourselves fiercely, completely, protectively—but without condition or compulsion. We cultivate it by following the Book of Mormon's advice to "invite all to come unto [Christ] and partake of his goodness, and [deny] none that come unto him, black and white, bond and free, male and female."[1] In celebrating and nurturing the divine spark in others, we discover that "all are alike unto God." Such spiritual fruit is sweet beyond imagining. And its taste transforms a group of people united by accidents of birth and geography into a holy commonwealth, a voluntary community of radical reformers, a holy hill of Zion. Again. And again.

NOTES

1. See 2 Nephi 26:33, Book of Mormon.

Silver Linings Playgroup

by Stephen Carter

STEPHEN is the editor of *Sunstone*, a magazine covering Mormon experience, scholarship, issues, and art. Stephen co-authors the award-winning graphic novel series "iPlates," which tell the stories of the Book of Mormon in comic-book form. He recently became a dance-team dad.

U rie, Wyoming. Population: 262.

Actually, 263. A baby had recently been born into our family. And I was her stay-at-home dad while her mom taught school.

Wyoming isn't really made for stay-at-home dads. It's an empty, windy, baby-unfriendly sage land strung with barbed wire and dolloped with cow pies. The men work in the fields, the oilrigs, or the mines. The women work with the house, the children, the animals. Or they're at playgroup.

The only reason I know this is because I saw them one fall day at the park across from the high school. I had brought my eighteen-month-old daughter to work off a little energy. About five moms were gathered at a picnic table talking while their kids played.

I knew them all. They were from my ward. But none of them seemed to recognize me.

Being the adrenaline junkie she is, my daughter quickly developed a game on the play equipment apparently called "run to the end of the catwalk and stop yourself from falling six feet to the ground by grabbing the bars."

Despite my best efforts, the inevitable soon happened. She missed the bars, fell, and landed on her shoulder. I ran to her, thinking that I would have to take her to the hospital forty minutes away. I picked her up as she screamed, carried her to the car, and drove away. None of the women there, each of whom saw me every week at church, ever inquired about the incident—or ever said more than "hi" when we sat in the same circle at "Moms and Tots" hour at the library.

Then we moved to a suburb in Utah County, otherwise known as Mormon country. We had a tree-lined street to wander, retaining walls to balance on, leaves to collect, gutters to wade. We became the most predictable part of the neighborhood, trawling the sidewalks day in and out.

And there was a ward playgroup.

But nobody thought to tell us about it. So my baby and I wandered the neighborhood alone for two years.

Finally, one day, as I was walking into my house, I saw a familiar pair coming down the sidewalk: a little blonde girl and her mom, both of whom I knew from my daughter's toddler Sunday School class. As I turned to shut the door, my imagination presented me with a quick preview of another few years of lone street wandering. In desperation, I turned around and called out to them. Just in case. My daughter came into the front yard and started playing with the little girl. The mom (we'll call her Anna) and I sat down and tentatively tried out a thing called "neighborly conversation."

Our daughters played together for two hours. Meanwhile, Anna told me that the leader of the ward playgroup had recently let it go inactive because her children were all in school now. So we decided that we'd put together a playgroup of our own.

I hosted the first playgroup at my house. I figured we'd start outside since it was such a nice spring day. I set up a day tent and cleaned out the sandbox, pumped up the beach ball and trimmed the rosebushes. And just in case, I whipped the inside of the house into shape; I wouldn't want anyone to look in the windows and think I was a bad housekeeper.

Anna and her daughter couldn't make it that day. One mom sent her husband, who happened to have the day off of work, when she heard I was hosting. One more mom came with her kids. Two dads, one mom, half a dozen kids. It went well until the kids wanted to go inside to play. The mom would not go in with us and herded her children toward home. She was blunt about her reason. "I'm married, so it wouldn't be right for me to be alone with another man, even if there are kids around."

It wasn't a surprising statement, but it still stung. It was what the women in Wyoming were likely thinking. It was probably what the woman who had sent her husband to the playgroup was thinking. Most Mormons can recall a story church president Spencer Kimball told about driving alongside a female Relief Society president who was walking home in the rain, shouting out encouragement, because even being in the same car for a moment or two with a woman other than his wife would be improper.

I was worried when fall rolled around. My daughter and I had really enjoyed the playgroups, and all of them had been held outdoors because of . . . well . . . the fact that I was male. It was nice to finally have friends and a little social time. But soon the option of holding playgroups outdoors would be gone, and with it, my welcome.

It was an unseasonably warm fall, and so the day after the 2012 election, we were playing at a nearby park. I was talking with one mom by the play equipment while Anna and another mom were pushing their kids on the swings. I could hear their conversation building to a minor crescendo. A moment later, the mom followed her son away from the swings over to us. She leaned in and whispered, "How in the *world* could someone vote for Obama *twice*?"

I looked over and saw Anna standing alone at the swings, her back toward us. When my daughter zipped by, I grabbed her and led her over. I hoisted her into the swing next to Anna's girl and started to push.

"Don't tell anyone this," I said. "But I voted for Obama twice, too."

When winter finally hit, Anna surprised me even more than she did when she first suggested the playgroup. She went out of her way to set up winter playgroups at the mall and in the church cultural hall. She made sure there was a space where I was still invited.

We've since moved away from that neighborhood, but we still go play with Anna and her daughter twice a week. Sometimes it's at a park, sometimes it's at a pool, and sometimes it's inside one of our houses. It's good to have friends.

I give unto you a parable.

A man and his daughter were playing by the side of the road. And they were lonely.

And lo, some Mormon women from Wyoming came upon them as they walked with their children, and they crossed to the other side of the road.

And behold, some Mormon women from Utah County came upon them as they walked with their children, and they crossed to the other side of the road.

But then came there a Democrat. And behold, she looked upon them with compassion, and she and her daughter sat down and played with them.

Building a Latter-day Zion
by Camille Fronk Olson

CAMILLE FRONK OLSON is a professor of Ancient Scripture at Brigham Young University and currently serves as chair of the Department of Ancient Scripture. She completed a PhD in Sociology—Middle East, a master's degree in Near Eastern Studies, and a bachelor's degree in Education. She has published on gospel scholarship, women in the scriptures, LDS/evangelical dialogue, LDS doctrine, and Palestinian families in the West Bank and Gaza Strip.

E ven though the specific theme of "Zion" is not often addressed by Mormon authorities today, the hope of building a Zion-like society is shared by members of the Church of Jesus Christ of Latter-day Saints worldwide. The doctrine is kept alive through its oft-repeated mention in scripture and Mormons' diligence in studying holy writ. Collectively, these scriptural directives and descriptions inspire success to build a compassionate, selfless, and progressive society through the power of Jesus Christ and his prayer that we be "one" as he and his Father are "one."[1] When such unity is realized, I picture a wholeness and congruity in every meaningful aspect of life, first in individuals and then to the larger community. Drawing from teachings and descriptions from the Book of Mormon, I share my vision of how a modern-day Zion would transform the world.

Economics. For nearly two centuries, one of the peoples of the Book of Mormon, the Nephites, succeeded in building Zion in which the people "had all things in common among them; therefore there were not rich or poor."[2] Their society was not made up of the "haves" and the "have nots," but they worked together to create a mutually beneficial society based on strong families and a strong work ethic.[3] Their earlier prophet-teachers instructed the Nephites to "be free with your substance, that [others] may be rich like unto you;"[4] to "succor those that stand in need of succor . . . and ye will not suffer that the beggar putteth up his petition to you in vain, and turn him out to perish."[5] The scriptural account records that at times they succeeded: "they did impart of their substance, every man according to that which he had, to the poor, and the needy, and the sick, and the afflicted; and they did not wear costly apparel, yet they were neat and comely."[6] In short, the economic goal for Zion is not fixated on "buying and selling," the perk that Satan threatens to remove from those who don't receive his "mark."[7] Rather, Zion aims to afford to everyone the needed educational opportunities and resources to make meaningful contributions. I imagine a modern-day Zion society where we liberally share our means and educational opportunities with others, whether they desire to build a Zion society or not, remembering that God is the true source of all that we have been given.

Politics. In their Zion society, the Nephites are described as having "no contentions and disputations among them, and every man did deal justly one with another."[8] More specifically, "there were no envyings, nor strifes, nor tumults, nor whoredoms, nor lyings, nor murders, nor any manner of lasciviousness; . . . there were no robbers, nor murderers."[9] Without the exorbitant costs of war, prisons, and security systems, such surpluses could be applied to expanding resources and improvements to benefit the entire society. To further promote harmony and mutual understanding, there was no differentiation of individuals or families by race or ethnic background (described as "nor any manner of ites") in the Book of Mormon.[10]

This remarkable social compatibility even existed for a time earlier in Nephite history when the believers were surrounded and interspersed by societies that did not embrace these values. This, to me, is therefore the most striking example of Zion in the Book of Mormon; it is possible to build many aspects of Zion in the world in which Mormons currently live, a world where devotion to God is increasingly distrusted and demeaned. In this earlier era, I sense the need for both liberality and conservation, or sharing our abundance freely and all laboring "every man [and woman] according to his strength."[11] Zion represents to me all that is good in liberalism and conservatism without the ugly trappings of idleness, elitism, gluttony, greed, and selfishness. Recognizing their abundant blessings from God, "they did not set their hearts upon riches; therefore they were liberal to all, both old and young, both bond and free, both male and female, whether out of the church or in the church, having no respect to persons as to those who stood in need."[12] In other words, the only distinction they made within their diverse society was who was in need for whatever reason.

Even one of the earlier government leaders, King Benjamin, sensed that he was not greater than his people, but a fellow servant and laborer. In his final speech to account for his actions as their king, he reported, "And even I, myself, have labored with mine own hands that I might serve you, and that ye should not be laden with taxes, and that there should nothing come upon you which was grievous to be borne—and of all these things which I have spoken, ye yourselves are witnesses this day."[13] Zion politics views every individual to be of value to society and gives to each the benefit of the doubt, whether or not one shares the same religion, capacity to contribute, or ancestry.

Because I live in a state that has very little diversity in political affiliation, those who align themselves with the minority party often feel marginalized, misunderstood, or rebellious. At the same time, some of those who identify with the majority party exacerbate the divide by claiming that no true believer in the gospel of Jesus Christ could support the other party with a clear conscience. The Zion I envision would welcome diverse perspectives fostered through politics that are also compatible with gospel principles. Consideration and meaningful dialogue on the ramifications of legislation on various segments of the population would allow for better solutions to evolve because of the candid and thoughtful discussions that would occur. Zion does not excuse individuals from critical thinking, but allows for more informed and humble discourse that necessitates genuine listening to those with opposing views.

Loyalty and Devotion to God. The secret to success in both economic and political unity is individual and collective reverence for God and his teachings "because of the love of God which did dwell in the hearts of the people."[14] "They did walk after the commandments which they had received from their Lord and their God, continuing in fasting and prayer, and in meeting together oft both to pray and to hear the word of the Lord."[15] During times of intense persecution from those who elected a different lifestyle, "they were steadfast and immovable in keeping the commandments of God, and they bore with patience the persecution which was heaped upon them."[16] They had made a covenant with God to "bear one another's burdens, that they may be light; . . . and . . . mourn with those that mourn; yea, and comfort those that stand in need of comfort."[17] The heart of Zion is authentically embracing and nurturing the love of God in our own souls to enable us as Mormons to treat others with "the pure love of Christ."[18]

When we willingly obey God because we love him, we more perfectly love our neighbors. Rather than collecting evidence to distrust them, we listen to them to understand their real intent. For me, a Zion society would allow me to speak of my beliefs and hopes for the world without fear of being misquoted, misunderstood, or misrepresented. More important than hearing what I want to hear from others to thereby produce a sensational story, I would ask questions to better understand, know, and honor those around me. In all my authentic interactions with others, I would underscore my devotion to my God and religion.

What Zion is Not. Building Zion as a united, congruent social, economic, and political society, however, does *not* necessitate the absence of those hostile toward the cause of Zion, or being in one specific location, or always agreeing about everything. Zion-like communities can emerge anywhere on the earth, wherever enough individuals collectively embrace a love for God's laws of honesty, duty, obedience, mercy, and charity toward others. Each community will communicate its own unique flavor for applying divinely inspired principles for building Zion. According to the Book of Mormon, God gathers his covenant people to one of many "lands of . . . inheritance" where they can build up Zion.[19] Even when the Nephites were oppressed, when they lived in crime-ridden societies with "quarrelings, . . . murderings . . . [and] plunderings" in the middle of a long war, they were able to create a sense of Zion in their hearts and families to the extent that "there never was a happier time among the people of Nephi."[20]

In truth, evidence of some tension or opposition accompanies or inspires successful attempts to build Zion. The fact that there were "disputations among the people" over what they should call Jesus Christ's church led loving, obedient Nephites to pray, ponder, and discuss before the Lord gave them the answer.[21] Variant opinions among a Zion people creates an environment for critical thinking and an informed discussion where better solutions become apparent and misunderstandings are swept away. The intent is to decide not who is right and who is wrong but rather what does my suggestion lack that another's suggestion supplies.

Experiences that remind us that we need each other and awareness that we are all in some way broken and in need of the saving power of Jesus Christ refresh the essential quality of humility and gratitude in a Zion society. Zion does not eliminate sin or the need for repentance and forgiveness; it creates an ideal learning environment to know how we can be healed. After describing the Nephites at a time they were obedient to the commandments and ordinances of God, "continually watchful unto prayer, relying alone upon the merits of Christ" and meeting often together to fast and pray, one of their leaders explained that when one of their numbers committed some iniquity, they were brought before church leaders and taught how to repent in order to again be a contributing member of the community.[22]

Whether our struggle is with some sort of addiction, be it drugs, alcohol, sex, or food; owning and embracing our religious history;

working through confusion over sexual orientation, self-loathing, or depression; or any one of a myriad of challenges that I or anyone faces in this fallen world, building Zion fosters faith and hope in deliverance. King Benjamin taught his people to acknowledge their divine indebtedness, asking, "Are we not all beggars? Do we not all depend upon the same Being, even God, for all the substance which we have, for both food and raiment . . . And behold, even at this time ye have been calling on his name and begging for a remission of your sins. And has he suffered that ye have begged in vain? Nay, he has poured out his Spirit upon you, and has caused that your hearts should be filled with joy."[23]

Finally, a successful Zion community in my mind would not be one where every question finds a satisfactory answer. Living in an environment where there are no more questions would soon squelch any thirst for learning and growth and foster arrogance. Accepting that "man doth not comprehend all the things which the Lord can comprehend" and that only "God knoweth all things strengthens the cords that bind us to Jesus Christ as the only way to salvation.[24] I would therefore imagine Zion to be a community where people equally value learning through study (research, scientific methods, pondering, experiments, etc.) as well as through faith (revelation through prophetic word, personal prayer, and inspiration). Only by applying both methods of learning do we finally recognize all learning is made possible through spiritual gifts from God.

I have sensed glimpses of what I imagine Zion to be like. One such setting was a ward in downtown Salt Lake City. The bishop was a retired truck driver who dutifully canvassed the three-block area of our ward boundaries, inviting every person he met to join us at Church on Sundays. Ward members came from diverse backgrounds: a significant percentage were in need of welfare assistance from the Church; several residents from the drug-rehabilitation center located around the corner attended regularly; and a member of the First Presidency of the Church lived within the ward boundaries and often was present for the main Sunday services. Non-traditional clothing and hairstyles, various accents, and contrasting levels of education were commonplace and welcomed. The result was a united community built on respect, compassion, and a universal need for healing that comes only through the Atonement of Christ.

For me as a practicing member of The Church of Jesus Christ of Latter-day Saints, the essence of Zion is communities or families or individuals all over the world who show their faith in Jesus Christ by the compassionate and hardworking way in which they live. Zion bespeaks unselfishness, gratitude, contentment, service, and a keen desire for lifelong learning to build a better tomorrow for those of future generations. Zion is about being one with Jesus Christ; it is about inviting his love to inform my attitudes and desires. Zion is becoming pure in heart through the redeeming power of Jesus Christ—one person at a time.

NOTES

1. John 17:21.
2. 4 Nephi 1:3, Book of Mormon.
3. 4 Nephi 1:7, 11, Book of Mormon.
4. Jacob 2:17, Book of Mormon.
5. Mosiah 4:16, Book of Mormon.
6. Alma 1:27, Book of Mormon.
7. Revelation 13:16–17.
8. 4 Nephi 1:2, Book of Mormon.
9. 4 Nephi 1:16–17, Book of Mormon.
10. 4 Nephi 1:17, Book of Mormon.
11. Alma 1:26–29, Book of Mormon.
12. Alma 1:30, Book of Mormon.
13. Mosiah 2:14, Book of Mormon.
14. 4 Nephi 1:15, Book of Mormon.
15. 4 Nephi 1:17, Book of Mormon.
16. Alma 1:26, Book of Mormon.
17. Mosiah 18:8–9, Book of Mormon.
18. Moroni 7:47, Book of Mormon.
19. See 1 Nephi 22:12; 2 Nephi 10:7; 3 Nephi 5:26; 29:1, Book of Mormon.
20. Alma 50:21–23; see also 1:25–30, Book of Mormon.
21. 3 Nephi, 27:1–7, Book of Mormon.
22. Moroni 6:4–8, Book of Mormon.
23. Mosiah 4:19–20, Book of Mormon.
24. See Mosiah 4:9 and 2 Nephi 9:20, Book of Mormon.

Inhabiting Zion
by William Morris

WILLIAM MORRIS is the founder of the Mormon literature and culture blog A Motley Vision and the co-editor of the fiction anthology *Monsters & Mormons*. His fiction and reviews have appeared in *Dialogue—A Journal of Mormon Thought, Irreantum,* and *BYU Studies.* He lives in Minnesota with his wife and daughter.

For more than a hundred years Mormons have clung to what I call the Orson F. Whitney approach to Zion. Whitney articulated this approach in his 1888 sermon/essay "Home Literature" where he said Mormons need to become a Zion people by creating their own culture, and that by doing so, Mormons "will yet have Miltons and Shakespeares of our own."[1]

At the time Whitney was promoting the aesthetic principles that make him the father of Mormon literature, Mormonism was coming to grips with the fact that Zion (then often defined as Utah) would need to reintegrate into Babylon (considered the wider world, sometimes defined more directly as the greater United States of America) if it was going to survive. Brigham Young's experiment in political, economic, and cultural isolationism had failed, and the rest of America had caught up to the Mormons. Zion was established in the mountaintops, but the mountains were no longer the State of Deseret—they were now the State of Utah, fully subject to the forces of U.S. federalism and American culture.

A new, less isolationist approach was needed, and for Whitney, the solution was for Mormons to produce culture of such power and genius that the gentiles (or non-Mormons) would have no choice but to recognize us an admirable, worthy people.

The cultural movement that Orson F. Whitney championed was paralleled by changes to LDS Church organization. If we Mormons were going to have to be in the wider world, we might as well get along with that world as best we could. Zion was to be built in its stakes (organizations of large Mormon communities), which would then seek to establish Zion in the hearts and homes of each member of the Church. That movement began with the end of polygamy and the secularization of Utah political and economic power, and consolidated with the administration of Heber J. Grant. It gained steam with the effort to correlate histories and theology into one easily digestible and translatable curriculum and the post-World War II outmigration of Mormons from the Intermountain West and internationalization of the Church. It eventually reached its apex during the administration of President Gordon B. Hinckley in the 1990s through the early 2000s. Finally, it seemed, Mormons were accepted—even if not fully understood.

That trajectory of acceptance came to a halt in the mid-2000s. And yet American Mormons of all political stripes still seem to think that acceptance by whichever right-left spectrum socio-cultural faction they prefer is possible, and that the solution is to continue to court respectability.[2] Others have determined isolationism is the answer. Neither option gets Mormons closer to Zion. Respectability is a sucker's game; isolationism is for 'fraidy cats. Respectability changes us too much; isolationism not enough.

This became clear to me during Mitt Romney's first presidential campaign when I read yet another opinion piece concern-trolling Romney's Mormonism. I can't remember which opinion piece or who wrote it—either in the *New York Times* or *Slate Magazine* or *The New Yorker* or some other East Coast equivalent.

But I do remember my reaction.

I was like, wait a second: I went to your schools. I read your books and magazines and alt-weeklies. I listened to your music. I watched your dramedies and sitcoms. I absorbed your vocabularies and theories. I bought your products. I voted for your politicians. I'm (almost) fully, freakin' assimilated, baby. I'm a GenX, post-punk, po-mo-Mo. I can walk your walk. Talk your talk. Snark your snark. Deconstruct your deconstructions. And this is what I get? This is my choice? To fulfill the trope of Mormons as either nice, hardworking model minorities or prudish, weird, irrational religionists? To ally myself with conservatives who refuse to see us as Christian, who support us only so long as we toe the party line? Or align myself with liberals who are only cool with us if we distance ourselves from belief and activity in the Church?

Yes, I'm vastly oversimplifying things. But that's because I remember how oversimplified the discourse about Mormonism was during the first time Mitt Romney ran for the Republican presidential nomination—the first "Mormon Moment"—and how it was even more farcical (albeit slightly more baroque) the second time around.

In the twenty-first century it was most visible in the political sphere, but such oversimplification has always been rampant in the cultural sphere. While Mormons may have never been the violent, oversexed Orientalized villains they were portrayed as in the early pulp fiction era, the new set of tropes which cast Mormons as nice, hardworking, reliable, naïve, conservative semi-Christians was not much better, even if the Mormon Church leadership often felt comfortable playing into them.

At around this time, I was instant messaging with my sister Katherine about all the Romney campaign coverage and the American Mormon desire for respectability and acceptance and she wrote something that resonated: "So, really, what's the point of denying our culture when it's not buying us anything anyway?" Whatever cultural currency we seemed to be able to gain through our Mormon-ness required either playing along with the new "nice Mormon" tropes or turning our Mormonism solely into an exotic cultural background, something that could spark a conversation so long as it was made clear that you no longer were an actual believer. I'd felt the pull of deep engagement with Mormon culture ever since I first discovered Mormon literature and began to see myself as a Mormon-American, a hyphenated citizen of a multicultural state. But that conversation unlocked a deeper yearning. A yearning that could be best described as a longing for Zion. I wanted to experience something as powerful as the feelings for Zion expressed by those early Saints who were carving it from the landscape.

But where is the Mormon Zion in the twenty-first century? The Mormon Church currently teaches it is to be found in and built through the sacred trinity of home-chapel-temple. I believe that. And I understand the Church's primary goal needs to be to preserve and improve those spaces. But it isn't always enough. Or at least it isn't for me. My worry is, as powerful as those spaces may be, they can't fully compete with the immense forces of the ideologies and –isms that would colonize our hearts and minds and wallets. The modern incarnation of the Mormon Church operates as a corporation because that's what it needs to be in order to be a multinational, multilingual, multi-unit organization. The gospel is the gospel, but within the organization, messaging and delivery has always been dependent on the socio-political and economic modes of the time. This dependency—this need for correlation and conformity—leads to gaps. Perhaps it shouldn't. If we were a perfect people, it wouldn't. We're not perfect.

Mormons are, however, still peculiar. The first decade-plus of the twenty-first century has been a reminder of that. And that's where Mormonism's hope for Zion lies: in augmenting the Zion spaces of home-chapel-temple by embracing peculiarity through the medium of culture. Not culture that follows the Orson F. Whitney model of seeking validation, of worrying about when our Shakespeares and Miltons will arrive. Rather culture—art—that allows individuals to be more fully Mormon in the world. Mormons need things (experiences, narratives, pieces of material culture, things lovely and of good report) we can carry with us when we're away from our sacred spaces in addition to those things that can strengthen their sacralization. We need to feel and experience Mormonism as an identity separate from all the –isms and do so without falling into zealotry or naive utopianism. We need to be able to negotiate our various roles and identities in ways that preserve in our hearts and minds a sense of Zion, of being peculiar. We need to plunder the rest of the world for all that's good and interesting and cool and leaven both the world and our own communities with culture that richly and fully expresses the Mormon experience and the experience of all the various sorts of Mormons.

Art—good art—creates a space inside us and among us that can resist all the vapid, insidious narratives that would take away our agency. It also can create a safe space to explore diversity of experience, belief, and worldview. Most importantly, unlike other discourses, it can exist among and amidst and in productive tension with official LDS Church discourse and practice.

It can, but so often it does not. Too often the Mormon people settle for culture that is powerful but not Mormon or Mormon but not powerful; has the form, but denies the power thereof. I'm not sure why. Especially since, while their numbers may be few, there are wonderful works of art that are both powerful and Mormon; there are experiences that can provide the feeling of being part of Zion. Of this I'm confident. Of this I, personally, testify:

It's sitting in a dark theater in San Francisco's Castro district filled with punks and Mormons and Mormon punks and viewing Greg Whitely's Arthur Kane documentary *New York Doll* and experiencing where the Mormons laugh and where the punks laugh and where we all shed tears. And then the heartbreak on the way out as I silently witness one of the punks grab Whitely's arm and thank him and reveal that he is a gay Mormon estranged from his family.

It's wearing a black t-shirt with white lettering that displays the name of my Mormon literature and culture blog in the Deseret Alphabet.

It's reading submissions to the *Monsters & Mormons* anthology and experiencing a sudden welling of pride and tenderness and awe at the way this group of Mormons have so fully embraced expressing their love of Mormonism and of the genre of fiction and in so doing create something wonderful, powerful, and new.

It's attending a crèche exhibit at the local Mormon chapel and at the end encountering Brian Kershisnik's painting *Nativity*. Or walking into the Oakland Temple Visitor's Center and stumbling across an exhibit of the paintings of Annie Henry and being reminded of the Romanian Orthodox icons I fell in love with on my mission.

It's holding hands with my wife in a theater in Dinkytown surrounded by Minneapolis hipsters watching Alan Sparhawk and Mimi Parker of the band Low sing indie rock hymns in harmony.

It's that moment when I'm writing a story and all my reading of literary fiction and/or science fiction meld with some aspect of LDS history, doctrine, thematics, material culture, or personal experience to create a moment that feels authentically Mormon. That click where all the aspects of my identity are feeding off each other and working together and the Spirit and my spirit rejoice.

It's the delight of seeing befuddled critical reactions to the erotics of abstinence in Stephenie Meyer's Twilight Series and to the goofy authenticity of Jared and Jerusha Hess's *Napoleon Dynamite*. It's Brandon Sanderson playing with deification in a series of epic fantasy novels. Or Ally Condie drawing on Utah landscapes and flora in a dystopian young adult trilogy. Or even Steven Peck writing about AIs who want to become Mormon and Eric James Stone writing about giant gas creatures who already are.

It's all this. But we need more. I need even more. We need more because what works for me may not work for other Mormons. And we need better. Maybe not Shakespeare and Milton better. Who needs that pressure? Who needs that respectability? But better as in: more full of craft, of thoughtfulness, of courage, of sacrifice, of love. More, more better and more good: more Mormon.

If Zion is going to survive not just as concept, but as an actual lived experience in twenty-first-century Mormonism, it needs to find a way to create spaces in which to exist. Our physical spaces may be mostly constrained to home-chapel-temple. Our presence in the public sphere may be dismissed, distorted, or denied. But in our hearts and minds and spirits there are spaces to be filled. What do we as a people want to fill them with? We may no longer be inhabitants of Zion, but Zion can inhabit us.

NOTES

1. First delivered as a speech by Bishop Orson F. Whitney at the Y.M.M.I.A. Conference, June 3, 1888, and subsequently published July 1888 in *The Contributor*. See http://mldb.byu.edu/homelit.htm, accessed June 2014.

2. There's nothing wrong with finding common ground with others, but becoming socially acceptable by downplaying your cultural background and/or conforming to how the broader culture think that it is acceptable for you to act given your cultural background is a problematic way of engaging with the world. Becoming acceptable is not the same as being accepted. This struggle is, of course, not unique to Mormons, although it is complicated by Mormonism's status as a young religion and an emerging culture.

Finding the Waters of Mormon
by Neylan McBaine

NEYLAN MCBAINE is the founder and editor-in-chief of the Mormon Women Project, a continuously expanding digital library of interviews with LDS women from around the world found at www.mormonwomen.com. Founded in 2010, the MWP has published nearly 300 interviews with women in twenty-two countries. As a writer, Neylan has appeared in *Newsweek, The Washington Post*, Patheos.com, and *Dialogue: A Journal of Mormon Thought,* among others. Her recent book, *Women at Church: Magnifying LDS Women's Local Impact,* drew on hundreds of interviews and years of study. Neylan works professionally as a strategist and account planner. She is a native New Yorker, lifelong Mormon, graduate of Yale University and mother of three literarily-named daughters.

When I was fifteen years old, I attended a regional youth conference at a YMCA campground in upstate New York on a frigid February weekend. Young women and young men tramped through the snow, memorializing the march of the Mormon pioneers, singing pioneer hymns from little paper booklets made to look like distressed leather. At one activity, we were given Oreos, only to discover they were filled with white toothpaste. We laughed so hard we cried as we tried to spit out the deceptively smooth paste, although we learned the intended lesson about Satan being cunningly deceptive. We returned to toilet-papered cabins and nervous preparations for an evening dance. The next morning, we bore our testimonies and learned of the Savior's love for us. "I think I feel angels around us," I whispered to my best friend beside me. "It feels like heaven," she replied.

Now that I am an adult, I understand just how much work went into preparing those activities and dances and testimony meetings and I am in awe of the leaders who cared so much about the development of my testimony that they went to elaborate efforts to create conditions where it could take root and flourish. I remain grateful for that brief glimpse of what seemed to me—an only child of separated parents from the middle of Manhattan—to be a little slice of heaven. Even though the salsa music wasn't what I would have picked for the dance and the food at the camp left a lot to be desired, and even though I was self-conscious around the boys and frozen to the bone, the feeling of love and unity overwhelmed it all.

I've hung on to that feeling in the intervening years and used it as a north star to gauge other attempts at creating Zion-like gatherings here on earth. Even though I've had moments with my family that are blessedly released from the terrestrial world, few communal efforts have ever reached that same plane where unity trumps all. I know it is attainable and I know it is real, and that knowledge drives much of the work that I do as a public voice for women in the Church today.

The quest for Zion today has dramatically shifted from the nineteenth-century call to have people gather to Utah from around the globe. At the Church's beginnings, physical threats made necessary a physical response: a gathering of bodies, of families, of believers, in a specific place. But the reality of twentieth- and twenty-first-century life has demanded instead a different kind of gathering: a gathering of minds and hearts to defend against unseen challenges, competing ideologies and emotional assailants. It is a virtual gathering, to answer a virtual world. In my work with women, I have seen members of the Church wrestle with what I believe is the essential question of our discipleship today: How do we maintain spiritual unity across the wide spectrum of cultures, political leanings, experiences and convictions that make up the church body today?

Mormonism is today an unsplintered religion, defined by the single embrace of a single institution. A recent trip to a Baptist church reminded me how unusual it is to have central governing bodies at the local, regional, and general level working hand in hand to oversee a global community. We do not have cultural designations or different descriptions of levels of orthodoxy, and I do not believe we can if we take seriously the Savior's warning: "I say unto you, be one; and if ye are not one ye are not mine."[1] Mormonism to my mind is not an ethnicity (although some have argued it is) in the sense that our familial line is not our tether to our spiritual inheritance. We are, rather, a "covenant people," suggesting it is making and keeping covenants that grafts us into the family of God, not a birthright. Even those born "in the covenant" must earn their own place through the making and keeping of individual commitments.

We are also not a hermetical religion. We do not siphon ourselves off from the cultural and educational influences of the world. We are people who are influenced by the forces around us. Where we draw the line between being in the world but not of the world varies from individual to individual, depending on family and national culture, personality, priorities, and convictions.

So we are left with the seemingly paradoxical task of embracing in a single family the vast collection of covenant-keeping people around the world, while celebrating the beauty and variety inherent in individual souls.

The question of how to achieve this wide embrace is the subject of my personal thinking and writing on the subject of women at church. For much of the twentieth century, technological limitations both in communication and travel meant that most of our female population was concentrated into a largely homogeneous body. The rise of "Molly Mormon" stereotypes—women devoted to at-home canning, quilting, and making their children's clothing—bore witness to the cultural and ideological unification that defined much of the past hundred years. For a Mormon woman of past decades, there was a sense of belonging in the community if she participated in culturally marking activities and philosophies. Today, however, our global membership demands that we not revel in what Mormon womanhood looks like, but, rather, what it feels like.

As we stretch toward a new identity of Mormon womanhood, our community craves a vision of how we can honor our priorities without being slaves to their former trappings. With a firm belief in the adage "You can't be what you can't see," I started the Mormon Women Project five years ago with the hope of offering a broader range of models for future Mormon women.[2] Could I widen our definition of a "good" Mormon woman by proving that intangibles, such as priorities and values, could still hold firm even if a woman wasn't canning and quilting? I like to think that because of the Mormon Women Project, our embrace has become a little wider, Zion a little closer.

In the Book of Mormon, we read about a group of people who follow the priest Alma into the wilderness to escape wicked King Noah. The group gathers at the Waters of Mormon to hear Alma preach the truth he himself has just learned, and follow Alma's example of being baptized. Alma teaches them "repentance, and redemption and faith on the Lord," and they rejoice in learning the truth. We learn that this people is "desirous to come into the fold of God, and to be called his people, and are willing to bear one another's burdens, that they may be light; yea, and are willing to mourn with those that mourn; yea, and comfort those that stand in need of comfort." Their commitment to and understanding of one another was so sincere that it was the "desire of their hearts" to support one another through life's darkest moments. That, for me, is Zion. It's the connection that comes from knowing there's a place for us in others' hearts. It's not all nodding heads in agreement with every statement uttered at church on Sunday. It's not all having treats, a song, and a lesson every Monday night in the Mormon tradition of a weekly family home evening. It's not about having everyone live in one place or dressing the same. The scriptures tell us the Waters of Mormon were "beautiful" to "the eyes of them who there came to the knowledge of their Redeemer."[3] The Waters of Mormon in my life have been every place, including that youth conference at the YMCA camp, where I came to the knowledge of my Redeemer. And my Zion is those literal and virtual places where covenants to support, love, comfort, and bear another's burden are being honored unrestrainedly and joyously.

My work with women in the church suggests to me we have far to go in ensuring every woman both desires to bear others' burdens and feels her own burdens are being borne by others. Zion requires both. Connection is reciprocal: the embrace is only wide if we ourselves add our outstretched arms to the circle, and it is only strong if we feel we can fall into the arms of others. We as a people are in the process of learning how to connect virtually today, apart from the physical proximity that defined most Zion communities of the past. We're breaking new ground, testing our cell towers' and fiber cables' ability to gather us in spirit rather than in body. We have work to do, but I'm confident our drive to embrace and be embraced will lead us one day to a place that is beautiful to our eyes, even if that place is as impalpable as the angels that will surround us.

NOTES

1. Doctrine and Covenants 38:27.
2. See http://www.mormonwomen.com/.
3. See Alma 18, Book of Mormon.

A Barrio Perspective on Building Zion in the Twenty-first Century

by Ignacio M. García

IGNACIO M. GARCÍA is the Lemuel Hardison Redd, Jr. Professor of Western and Latino history at Brigham Young University. He writes extensively about Chicano civil rights, politics, and sports. He served twice as bishop of Spanish-language wards and his forthcoming memoir about growing up Latino and Mormon is being published by Fairleigh Dickinson University Press.

Among Latino Mormons the term *barrio* means both the local neighborhood and the ward—the term for a Church of Jesus Christ of Latter-day Saints congregation. It is particularly meaningful for Latino Latter-day Saints that their local church is conceptualized as a neighborhood, because unlike many Utah congregations, LDS wards outside of Utah are not neighborhood churches. Few Latino spaces have the density of Mormons needed to create a neighborhood church; thus, the significance of a "conceptualized" religious neighborhood space for Latinos is greater than one may assume. This barrio space is also important in what it means for Mormonism in the twenty-first century.

I grew up in one such barrio in San Antonio, Texas. My ward served as a familial home for many disparate individuals, few of whom had extended Mormon genealogy or even Mormon friends in their local neighborhood. In that barrio-ward we had an extended family of friends—uncles and aunts, grandparents, and brothers and sisters who looked after us, counseled one with another, and even pulled our ears periodically—though no bloodlines linked us. Like all families, we argued, envied, sometimes shunned particular individuals, we often frustrated each other, but we also came together to worship, forgive, and even intermarry and merge as in-laws.

Because most had no extended Mormon roots, we depended on this extended partnership to keep focused in an often-hostile world. Our Mexican neighbors didn't always understand our religious choices, and sometimes, in the church we called ours, we were not seen as of the "right" lineage. In partial isolation, we learned to help one another navigate our neighborhoods, our jobs, and our public space as Mexican Mormons. Our local church was poor but collectively—and with some church resources—we had a chapel in which to worship, a cultural hall for gathering, and a parking lot in which we could hold carnivals or play sports. Being part of the Mormon community allowed us to step cautiously into the larger society. In the extended village of Mormonism, we found empathy from leaders and fellow saints, even as we sometimes experienced the unfortunate prejudices in both the religious and the public arena.

As a poor young boy with little expectation of a happy life, conversion was a lifesaver. In my ward is where I truly discovered I was of value. It was where I learned to dream, to hunger after learning, and where I acquired the social skills to navigate the larger world. Uncoordinated, I played church ball anyway; shy, I entered church speech festivals and acted in church plays. I learned to preach from the pulpit and conduct Boy Scout and priesthood meetings. More importantly I learned what it took to be a good leader and a good follower.

Growing up I felt secure, if not fully comfortable, within the all-encompassing world of Mormon doctrines and practices. It was still early, but even then, middle-class, nuclear-family focused, self-absorbed religiosity was beginning to creep into Mormonism, pushed along by a church fully committed to modernity and its capitalist culture.

By the time I became a bishop, this new style and focus was firmly the model for most of American Mormonism. Modern-lived Mormonism had become powerfully focused on the nuclear family. Most Latino wards, however, continue to function on a more communitarian pattern because we tend to be more attuned to the church's history and doctrine than the institutional process. In making this our focus, our version of Mormonism remains vibrant, forward-looking, proud of its own cultural and historical uniqueness, while still somewhat grounded in the church's traditions and culture.

Ironically, because of our focus, Latino Mormons challenge the faith. Our social and economic struggles demand the church prioritize people and community above structure and growth. Latinos are still often considered outsiders in wider American society, so our wards and stakes are places of refuge in ways they are not necessarily so for white Mormons. White Mormons tend to be more integrated into an American middle-class society that shares—at least on paper—many of their cultural and social values. When our local and regional leaders understand the challenges that we face in the larger society they make policies that help our wards flourish. When they do not, we flounder.

One of the main challenges for the church today is what to do with the large number of undocumented members and their immigrant cousins in Spanish-speaking wards that continue to grow in number but show no signs of evolving into traditional Mormons. For now, the church allows and even encourages this growth, making Latinos the fastest growing conversion group in the United States. When I was growing up, the church was less certain it wanted to keep us together and several attempts to integrate us into English-language wards were disasters, pushing many out of the church and forcing church leaders to reestablish Spanish-language units they had so recently abandoned. That policy has mostly been set aside, though periodically some local stake leader will experiment with forced integration, only to find it often as disastrous and detrimental today as it was in my youth.

Even with these considerations, integration into the core of Mormonism is essential for Latinos to become a vital part of the church's leadership and its institutional culture. Making full integration possible requires the faith to open to a kind of theology that respects no political or socio-economic boundaries and which views fellowship and brother/sisterhood as important as spiritual/religious order. This shift will require church leaders to assume that doctrinal strength will be sufficient, and their members' commitment to the church will be stronger than personal philosophies and habits.

Latino Mormonism, even with normal human weaknesses and flaws, offers a way forward. Social conditions and historical constructs make the Latino perspective more amenable to the communal notions of our faith's origins, while allowing for a sense of collective individualism. Latino Mormons want and need the creation of community to be fundamental to our faith. Most Latino Mormons come from first- or second-generation convert families. We live far from the LDS core—both physically and culturally—and our allegiance to the Mormon faith—which is often perceived as indifferent to our culture and our social needs—makes an extended community outside the church sometimes difficult to construct.

Mormonism's doctrinal—if not always theological—commitment to individual growth within a community allows Latinos to develop spiritual communities that strengthen the church. The Mormon notion of the extended family reaching upward to the heavens resonates with us, as does the concept of a "brothers/sister" communal concept of charity. Whether through Catholicism's catechism, the paternal political states they originate from, or simply from teachings of the Book of Mormon—the one scripture most Latinos embrace as their own—they see within Mormonism a religious *compadrazgo* that places familial commitment to an extended religious family as central to their spiritual life.

This stands in contrast to much of modern mainstream Mormonism's focus—some might even say obsession—on the nuclear genealogical family. Because of this constructed religious family that brings others from outside the immediate family inward, this *compadrazgo*—which functions as both a familial and communal relationship—can grow, evolve, and adapt to changing norms within the comfort of numbers, making it easier for Latino Mormons to accept changes in the faith's collective structure and doctrinal practices and not feel subsumed by them. Latino's extended familial Mormonism challenges the church to continue to move toward a focus on the dispossessed, the poor, the undocumented, and the un-integrated individual. It was the church's growth in the international arena and among U.S. Latinos that most likely led to the recent addition of a fourth mission to the Church's previous threefold mission: to minister to the poor and needy. That new mission can eventually lead Latter-day Saints to expand their vision beyond organizational loyalty and a checklist-style religiosity to one of genuine concern for others, regardless of social, cultural, and racial boundaries. This expanded vision—already part of the doctrine and historical practice—can also help open the church to less hierarchical governance, a non-corporatist culture at the top, and de-couple it from conservative politics that have held sway over a sizeable part of the membership in the United States.

Current Latino leaders at the general authority level do not provide a vision of Latino Latter-day sainthood much different than that of white leadership. There is no Hispanic ministry. There is no discussion of the particular needs of people of color, their history, or how they fit into the larger church—at least no discussion has been made public. Unfortunately in practice, Latino Mormonism currently contributes little to the wider practices of the church. Yet, newer and future Latino leaders—especially those raised in this country—are moving into the church leadership structure with firsthand knowledge of Latino poverty and the social challenges they face, and are doing so at a time when political and social progressive thought is taking hold among them. Even conservative Latino members are confronting discrimination in American society (and sometimes within the church) and so are also aware they are "different" and possibly "strangers" and in need of a theology that is more people-focused and less rigid when it comes to "navigating the outside world."

The potential growth of a Latino ministry is more likely at the local level, where leadership confronts issues closely related to economic, social, and legal realities of their members' lives. As a bishop, I was fully aware that poverty, undocumented status, and the lack of integration into the larger society often played a part in their participation in church. Most problems had economic or social foundations before they had a moral one. This is the case for most issues today, yet too many leaders perceive problems being as the result of a failure to be faithful.

Because many American Mormon leaders have weaned themselves on the American gospel of self-help and individual responsibility, few understand—often despite their best efforts—how to find a communal response to their members' challenges. Though the church is structured to promote a collective solution to most problems, too many priesthood and auxiliary responses rely on an individual's ability to solve their own problems with a few tips from church manuals or with a strong admonition to "choose the right."

Latino Saints are not any more enlightened than their white counterparts, but their political and social challenges have always required collective action; they are much more amenable to collective help. Fundraisers (garage sales, tamaladas, etc.), clothing exchanges, group prayer, resource-sharing, and the like are an integral part of the Latino Mormon life, while they have often faded among white urban Mormons. Latino leaders are more likely to preach member solidarity as more foundational to building Zion than their white counterparts, who see it being built one brick (individual family) at a time.

Latino Saints' solution to insensitive institutional and cultural practices within the church will eventually come as a collective one. Rather than fixate on personal rights in Zion, they will advocate for inclusive governance, a more expansive retelling of church history and the development of a theology that sees all of God's children as fully equal. They will need to do so because the institutional church, while evolving to meet the needs of its new converts, is still very much an institution that matured during (white) American power and prestige, where people of color had no historical or structural influence and still struggle to have one today.

If Latino wards do not succumb to the nuclear-family, self-actualization, and individual-salvation model of many traditional

Mormon wards, they can recapture the communitarian message of earlier Mormon teachings and add depth and richness to Mormon life. There will be support from other non-Latino Mormons who see the need to expand the church tent not only by increasing the racial, ethnic, and national diversity of its converts, but also by enlarging its cultural, intellectual, and social boundaries to create a diverse and yet more cohesive community

In my years in the church I have seen many Spanish-language units go from predominantly Mexican to diverse Latino wards, and this has forced an accommodation to multiple cultures and religious idiosyncrasies which is often lacking in traditional LDS wards. In the U.S. there are few more diverse spaces than Latino wards, where it's not uncommon for people from over fifteen countries to worship together. There are also a growing number of mixed Latino/white families who choose to attend Latino wards providing skills and knowledge while learning this cohesiveness. Latino Latter-day Saints have had to engage in a universal church in a way most white Mormons have not. Given their historical background, their diversity and their life experiences, Latinos can—if they retain this cohesive identity—contribute greatly to the church, even as they challenge it to remain focused on sustaining the Body of Christ. Treating our wards like our barrio can sustain us through the troubled waters of modernity by bringing the strengths of families and individuals for the benefit of the whole. The barrio is Zion.

Of Chicken Salad Sandwiches
Heather Bennett Oman

HEATHER BENNETT OMAN attended Boston University and received her bachelor's in Communication Disorders and then attended George Washington University where she received her master's in Speech Language Pathology. She is currently working toward combining her love of horses in therapeutic riding with speech and language therapy. She lives in Virginia with her husband Nathan and their two children.

On Fridays, I lunch with two girlfriends. They are new friends, which can be a rarity at age thirty-nine. We met through a volunteer organization, and we've known each other for less than two years. The friendship has grown slowly, over time, on a picnic bench, while lunching on chicken salad sandwiches from the nearby deli. I look forward to these lunches all week. Friday has officially become chicken salad sandwich day.

One day, we were talking about marriage. My friend has a twenty-year-old son who is engaged. She feels, understandably, trepidation about the marriage. "They are so young!" she lamented as she bit into her sandwich.

"Well, you never know. Age doesn't always matter. My two sisters got married when they were twenty, and they are still happily married," I told her, trying to be comforting.

My friend eyed me as she chewed, and then said, "But, correct me if I'm wrong, you're Mormon, and Mormons don't believe in premarital sex, right? I mean, that's a serious thing, right?"

I nodded and affirmed, "That's a serious thing."

"Then," she continued, carefully, "don't you think, that, well, you know, Mormons kind of, rush in because of the sex?"

I considered her question. She wasn't wrong. Mormons consider marriage to be highly important, and there is an expectation of not having premarital sex. And if you aren't having sex, indeed, a long engagement lasting years would be torturous.

So we talked about it. We talked about sex, marriage, and the covenants Mormons make in our temples about chastity before marriage and fidelity after. We talked about rules and religion in general. The conversation remained pleasant and lovely, because these women are my friends.

The topic came back around to personal decisions about religions, and my two ladies confessed that neither of them are particularly active churchgoers. The conversation turned serious, however, when one of my friends said, "I've looked and looked for a church. But until I can find one where I can walk in with my brother and the entire place will welcome him for who he is, I'll spend my Sunday mornings at home."

My friend's brother is gay.

She looked at me, her eyes asking the question. Is your church the place? Can I take my brother to your church and sit with you?

I looked back and said, "I wish, with all of my heart, that I could tell you that would happen at the Mormon Church. Your brother could sit with me, he could sit with my husband, and I know my bishop would welcome him as well. There are many, many Mormons I know who would be happy to see him. But I have to be honest, there are more than a few who would not."

She nodded, as if she expected that answer. And she thanked me for being honest. And I wondered if she had another question:

Why would you stay in such a church? And how could you expect others to join it?

But because she is my friend, and because chicken salad sandwich day is about enjoying the sunshine on a picnic bench while eating an excellent sandwich on a fat slab of bread with the perfect combination of salt and pepper and mustard, she didn't ask.

But it's a question I ask myself. Why would I stay in such a church?

Some days, I'm just not sure. Being a part of a community is sometimes hard, and people do things that I disagree with, or that I find appalling, or that just plain drive me nuts. Identifying with a culture can be difficult if you don't feel bonded or even want to associate with others who identify with that same culture. And people, Mormons too, can be hurtful. These are the days when I wonder, what am I doing here?

Most days, I know. I know why I stay, and I know why I think it's a good thing if other people join this church. My reasons are about heritage, truth, and my relationship with God.

Mormons take their heritage seriously. We have a giant genealogical library devoted to finding our heritage. We have family history centers all over the world devoted to finding our heritage. We are asked to hold family meetings where we search online tools and upload images and scan documents, all to record and preserve our heritage.

To a Mormon, heritage is not something to be taken lightly.

I grew up on stories of my pioneer ancestors, the men, women, and children who were forced to "walk across the plains" from Nauvoo, Illinois, to Salt Lake City, Utah. I've seen the piano that came "across the plains" in my great-great-grandfather's house, and marveled at the sheer force of will my great-great-grandmother must have exerted to convince her husband to drag that thing thousands of miles. As a child, I was engrossed in the story of my ancestor whose twins died in the winter of the crossing, and how she had to rip her shawl in half to make shrouds for each of them as she buried them in the snow, because they died "on the plains."[1]

"The plains" is a very big thing for Mormons.

I hear these stories, and I feel their weight. My sister was told once that our family has believing blood. I'm not exactly sure what it means, but I've repeated it to myself again and again. Believing blood. This heritage, this church, it's in my blood. It's who I am—even the parts I don't like. If I left, if I decided I couldn't be a part of this church, it would still always be a part of me. It's a gross cliché and I hate that, but I can't describe it any other way. I feel the sanctity of the sacrifices my ancestors made, and it makes the sacrifices I make now and the objections I have seem paltry. They sacrificed so much; it must have been for something great. I owe it to stay and discover and experience the greatness of their vision for this gospel.

I also happen to believe the gospel is true.

Joseph Smith was the founder of The Church of Jesus Christ of Latter-day Saints. Members of the Mormon church believe he is a prophet and believe he restored the ancient church in the modern days. We believe that, at age fourteen, he prayed in a grove of trees about which church he should join, and in answer to his prayer, he was visited by God the Father and his beloved son, Jesus Christ. We believe Joseph saw not just spirits, but physical manifestations of God and Jesus, and that Jesus told the young Joseph Smith he was not to join any church, but to start his own.

It is really, really easy to dismiss Joseph Smith as a raving lunatic.

Visions in the forest? Starting new churches? And the story gets crazier. Joseph Smith was then asked to dig up some plates made of gold hidden in a hill near his home. These plates supposedly contained a record of an ancient people written in an ancient language, and Joseph Smith, a poorly educated farmer from New York, translated the book and presented it as another testament of Jesus Christ.

Nobody does that and stays out of an asylum.

And yet, Joseph Smith did. Joseph Smith published that translation of that ancient record, a work members of our church call The Book of Mormon. Indeed, it's where we get the nickname "Mormon." This book remains much harder to dismiss than Joseph Smith's claim to have seen angels in the forest.

I'm not a historian, and I'm not a scholar. People smarter than I have examined the book from all sides. Some have proclaimed it unhistorical, that the events in the book couldn't possibly have happened according to the accepted timeline. Some have claimed the translation doesn't follow ancient patterns, or there are internal inconsistencies. I'm not sure what to make of the conflicting information about the book, but having read it several times, I know at the very least it's an amazing piece of literature. How could somebody with Joseph Smith's background have written it? It hardly seems possible. He either translated it through the power of God, or it's a lie. If it's a lie, it's a bold and audacious one, and Joseph Smith took an unfathomable risk in publishing it to build a new religion. He risked his family and his livelihood, and in the end, paid for the whole thing with his life.

I doubt most authors would die to preserve their work.

If I can't dismiss the Book of Mormon as fiction, then Joseph Smith must be who he said he was, a man chosen by God to bring a restoration of the ancient church back to the earth. If I believe the Book of Mormon to be the word of God, then I want to be a part of the community that is built around that word, even when that community does things that I don't love. I recognize truth in the doctrine, and so I stay.

Truth can't always overcome a community's shortcomings, though. A dear friend of mine suffers from severe cerebral palsy. He is confined to a wheelchair, his body unresponsive to his active and productive brain. He can't speak, and communicates through a system of eye blinks and head nods, aided by a computer system. I introduced him to the gospel, and he asked to learn more. I brought missionaries to his home, and they taught him the doctrine of the resurrection. They taught him his body would be made perfect in the next life. At first, I don't think he understood, but then we explained it again, that there would be a time in his eternal existence when he did not have CP. His whole face and body lit with light, and he pretty much said, "I *knew* it!" He recognized truth and his spirit confirmed it. He was baptized shortly thereafter.

About fifteen years after his baptism, I got a note from him explaining that he was no longer a member of the church. He didn't feel comfortable, he told me, and although he tried, he always felt like an outsider. So, he took his name off of the records of the LDS church and rejoined his family's old church. Mormons are clearly not unique in feeling the weight of religious heritage. And clearly we need to do a better job of expanding our welcome.

It is difficult to stay in a community if you don't feel loved or valued. Mormons face this problem a lot, as evidenced by my friend's story, and I have my own stories of of times I wondered where I fit into my church. Conflicts, offenses, false doctrine, and leaders with whom I don't agree have all contributed to thoughts of leaving the church and looking for acceptance and love elsewhere. It's a tempting prospect, especially on the days I come home from church feeling more battered than uplifted.

I have struggled with questions. If God wants us to believe in Him so much, why then do we see so little of Him? Why don't we all have visions as startling and clear as Joseph Smith? Why aren't we all visited by angels so we know of a surety that God is there? But I always come back, not only because of the heritage and the truth, but also because of the glimpses I've had of the Divine.

I cannot deny those glimpses. I've never seen an angel or a personage of light, but I have felt the clarity of mind and heart that comes with what Mormons call the teaching of the Holy Ghost. I have had thoughts come to me to act in such a way that ended up helping a friend—a thought I would not have had on my own. I have been led to circumstances I would not have chosen on my own, and spoken with words that I know were not mine. My relationship with God has not prevented me from having trials in my life, but through the trials I've felt a comforting and loving presence. After I had a miscarriage, I comforted my sobbing mother-in-law, telling her that I was feeling okay, and that I wanted her to feel okay too. She snapped back, "Of course you're feeling okay! The entire family is praying for you right now! Nobody thinks to pray for the grandmother!"

She wasn't wrong.

Because of my heritage, the doctrines I believe are true, and my small but undeniable experiences with God, I stay in this imperfect community. I stay in this church that many people don't understand or view with hostility. I acknowledge the shortcomings even as I pledge my loyalty and faith, because I believe, more than I have ever believed anything, that this is where God wants me to be. I believe it's where God wants everybody to be.

I wished I could tell all of these things to my friend as we finished our sandwiches and balled up our napkins and got ready to go. I'm not a very bold missionary, and I don't always feel comfortable proclaiming my faith with declarative sentences. Since she didn't directly ask me to defend my faith, I didn't. Instead I hugged her as we said goodbye, and hoped that she could feel my love for her, that through me should somehow also feel God's love for her and His love for her entire family. I hoped, for the moment, a show of love would be enough to convince her of the goodness that could be found in the Mormon church.

And the next Friday afternoon, we talked about politics instead.

NOTES

1. From 1846 through much of the nineteenth century, Mormons traveled "over the plains" of the Midwest, specifically Iowa, Nebraska, Kaansas, Colorado, Wyoming, and Utah, from Nauvoo, Illinois, and elsewhere to settle the Utah area. Many pioneers sacrificed their homes, possessions, and even their lives. These pioneers are honored today in many Mormon stories.

Zion as Salvation from Sartre's Heaven
by Nathan B. Oman

NATHAN B. OMAN was born in Salt Lake City, Utah. A lifelong Latter-day Saint, he cannot remember a time he did not attend Mormon meetings each week. He was educated at Brigham Young University and Harvard Law School and is currently a law professor at the College of William and Mary in Williamsburg, Virginia. One of his greatest ambitions in life is to play "Foggy Mountain Breakdown" on the banjo.

According to the French philosopher Jean Paul Sartre, "Hell is other people." Sartre's statement is more than a bit of Gallic misanthropy. Rather, it presents a particular ideal of what fully realized humanity should be. In theological terms, it presents an idea of salvation, what we might call salvation as the fully liberated individual. For Sartre, to live an authentic life is to live a life constituted by one's own unconditioned choices. Such a life is a singular moral achievement, one that requires not only the abandonment of self-deceptions that obscure responsibility for our choices, but also liberation from the conditioning force of human relations limiting individual choice. To live the best life is to live independently, a life constituted fully by one's own choices. Those choices, in turn, are at their most truly authentic when they are least contingent on our social roles and commitments.

Sartre's vision of the unconditioned and liberated individual is extreme. Its celebration of freedom, along with its anxiety about the threats to that freedom, however, captures a central moral and spiritual dynamic in the modern world, perhaps especially in the United States. The Declaration of Independence is a document about national self-determination. Strikingly, however, it speaks in individual rather than national terms. Thomas Jefferson did not justify the creation of the United States because the new American nationality demanded a new nation. Rather the Declaration of Independence points toward a trinity of life, liberty, and happiness. Less striking than Sartre's aphorism, Jefferson also presented a salvation of liberated individualism. Life's purpose is the pursuit of happiness, something that can only be achieved through individual freedom. Somewhat melodramatically, Jefferson declared, "I have sworn upon the altar of God eternal hostility against every form of tyranny over the mind of man."[1] Notice that the quest for freedom was far more transcendent than a political struggle for a particular legal regime of protective rights. Rather, Jefferson's ambitions extended to the liberation of individuals from the conditioning power of history, tradition, and all of the other habits and social networks that bind the freedom of "the mind of man."

Mormonism inverts the logic of the salvation of the fully liberated individual. In the revelations of Joseph Smith, the completely independent individual, far from being a beatified ideal, is either the condition from which one achieves salvation by escape into social relations or the damnation reserved for the exceptionally wicked in the future. The inversion begins with the radically individualistic Mormon account of human origins. In the theology of the Mormon church's restoration narrative, life does not begin with birth. Rather, we lived long before mortality in some heavenly realm with God. Indeed, ultimately Mormonism denies that human souls have origins in the sense of having a point of creation. In an 1833 revelation the Lord says, "Man was in the beginning with God. Intelligence, or the light of truth, was not created or made, neither indeed can be."[2] The universe of traditional Christian theology is essentially unitary, beginning with a single self-existent God who then calls into existence everything that is, including, crucially, our souls. In contrast, the Mormon uni verse is fundamentally pluralistic. God is self-existent, but he always finds himself amidst other self-existent beings, the eternal uncreated souls of humanity.[3] In its most metaphysically radical formulation, Mormonism asserts the human soul is ontologically independent of God. He did not make us. Rather, like him, our souls—or at least some primal choosing and thinking essence of our souls—have always existed. Our individuality is a fundamental feature of reality in the same way God is a fundamental feature of reality.

In a sense, we begin as liberated individuals. We start free and independent. A soul in this condition, however, has not achieved salvation. It is alone, alienated, and miserable. The restoration's story of salvation can be told as a prolonged effort to overcome and escape from unconditional freedom, not because of the terror of choice that Sartre castigated, but because unconditional freedom requires isolation. We are only truly free in the sense of being unconditioned when we are not subject to the pressure and coercion of human relationships. Central to the Mormon story of pre-mortality is a vast council of "the intelligences that were organized before the world was."[4] The self-existent souls came together and agreed to a plan, a collective project in which covenants and shared goals began to knit together previously isolated—but free—souls. In other words, we achieve salvation by overcoming our independence, escaping our primal alienation, and binding our souls together with the souls of others. To use the language of Mormon temple rituals, our goal is to "seal" souls together. Indeed, the final ambition of God's plan is to seal the whole human race together in a web of insoluble social connections.

The same idea can be seen in Mormon doctrines surrounding "the sons of perdition" and "outer darkness." Mormonism takes a very nearly universalistic approach to salvation. Almost everyone is to inherit a kingdom of glory in the hereafter. In Mormon cosmology, however, a special hell is reserved for those traitors known as the "sons of perdition," a tiny group who openly and knowingly betray God. Their fate is to spend eternity in "outer darkness." Tellingly, outer darkness is not a lake of fire and brimstone. Indeed, it is not a place of torments at all. Rather it returns damned souls to their primal condition of independence. Their hell is to live forever without Sartre's perdition of other people. Their misery consists of never knowing the encumbrances and limits imposed by the demands of relationships with others.

Scholars of religion generally describe the Mormon concept of Zion in terms of failed nineteenth-century utopianism. Joseph Smith founded Mormonism in a Jacksonian America bubbling over with new projects for human improvements. He was far from the only religious leader to re-imagine society in hopes of establishing a New Jerusalem. Mormons experimented with various systems of cooperative property arrangements and ideal communities. As they moved west, ultimately settling in Utah under Brigham Young, their social experiments became more grandiose. Ultimately, Brigham envisioned an independent Mormon commonwealth in the Great Basin characterized by religious unity, cooperative effort, egalitarian economic relations, and polygamous families. Even the alphabet and patterns of clothing were to be recreated for the Mormon Zion. (The Church archives in Salt Lake City house yellowing photographs of Brigham Young's daughters scowling at the camera as they model the so-called "Deseret costume." No one looks happy in nineteenth-century photographs, but I can't help but think that they look particularly unenthusiastic about their father's sartorial foray.) By the end of the nineteenth century, however, utopian Mormon independence and polygamy had to be abandoned, much to the relief of modern Latter-day Saints. Zion as a concrete utopia could not be sustained in the face of a massive wave of federal polygamy prosecutions, technological change that undermined geographic isolation, and the integrating force of expanding consumer markets.

When Zion is understood through the lens of nineteenth-century memories, the problem for Latter-day Saints is to make sense of what it means to build Zion in a post-utopian world. Mormons seem to have irrevocably committed themselves to participation in the modernity. We are not going to withdraw into the desert to build cooperative utopias. If Zion is a self-contained religious utopia, however, the willingness to live within modernity is a problem. It potentially reduces Zion to little more than a distant memory or perhaps a hoped-for millennial future, an exercise in nostalgia or eschatology. Alternatively, we might reimagine Zion in terms of modern social or political projects aimed not at utopia but at social justice or political righteousness of some kind. Seen in these terms, the nineteenth-century Mormon experience of Zion building becomes a set of stories to be mined for proof-texts aimed at persuading Mormons to support some contemporary political project. Rather than an exercise in nostalgia, it becomes a very peculiar form of political rhetoric.

Both nostalgia and the quest for contemporary social relevance miss the deeper work that Zion does in Latter-day Saint thought. Ultimately, Zion orients me toward the world and crucially toward how I understand my relationship to the claims of individualism and community. Seen in the context of Mormonism's cosmic story of primal individualism in search of redeeming social connection, Zion is not really about utopia. The cooperative efforts of nineteenth-century Mormons were but one reflection of an orientation toward the world that continues long after Brigham's dreams of a Mormon commonwealth have receded into history. In scripture, Zion appears less as a blueprint for social or economic reform than as an account of human salvation. In one of Joseph Smith's earliest additions to Mormon scripture, the ancient prophet Enoch preaches to a wicked world. Those who believe *on his words* come together to form a city. "And, lo, Zion, in process of time, was taken up into heaven. And the Lord said unto Enoch: Behold mine abode forever."[5] Joseph Smith made the same point in different language, teaching, "That same sociality that exist among us here will exist among us in the eternal worlds."[6] The implication is that the quality of the eternities hinges on the quality of our relationships. To build Zion is to dwell with God and crucially we dwell with God as a city, a collective defined by its sociability.

Zion is thus more than nostalgia for a string of failed nineteenth-century utopias. Rather it provides a way for thinking about individualism, community, and the good life. For me it teaches that independence and freedom are less an individual accomplishment than a basic human condition, a condition that threatens to provide us with nothing more than loneliness and alienation. Salvation, on the other hand, consists of deep and meaningful connections with other people. Indeed, family, friendship, and community offer us the only redemption in what would otherwise be an eternity of isolation. Zion is a way of orienting oneself in the world that is at odds with the ethos dominating much of the modern world. Both the rugged individual of the neoliberal right and the liberated iconoclast of the left appear in Zion as somewhat pathetic and alienated figures, sad souls struggling in their primal isolation, blind to what can ultimately save them. Likewise, the intensely social heaven toward which Mormons strive exalts cooperation, unity, love, and obligation in what can appear to the denizens of modernity as a suffocating priority of community over individual. Zion thus provides an orientation toward the world that will always create for me a certain feeling of being ill at ease in a culture as dedicated to the freedom of the individual as the United States. It has the virtue, however, of offering me salvation from the bleak heaven toward which Sartre pointed the modern world.

NOTES

1. Thomas Jefferson to Dr. Benjamin Rush, Monticello, September 23, 1800, *Papers of Thomas Jefferson,* 32:168.

2. Doctrine & Covenants 93:29.

3. See Abraham 3:23, The Pearl of Great Price.

4. Abraham 3:22, The Pearl of Great Price.

5. Moses 7:21, The Pearl of Great Price.

6. See Doctrine & Covenants 130:18.

Stretching Toward Stewardship and Surplus
by J. David Pulsipher

J. DAVID PULSIPHER is a history professor at Brigham Young University–Idaho. He earned a BA in American Studies from Brigham Young University, and a PhD in the same discipline from the University of Minnesota. David spent time as a visiting professor and Fulbright scholar at Jamia Millia Islamia in Delhi, India. His research focuses on the intersections of Mormon history and theology with just war, peace, and nonviolence traditions. His publications include *When We Don't See Eye to Eye: Using the Weapon of Love to Overcome Anger and Aggression,* "'Prepared to Abide the Penalty': Latter-day Saints and Civil Disobedience." With Patrick Q. Mason and Richard L. Bushman he co-edited *War and Peace in Our Time: Mormon Perspectives.* He and his wife, Dawn, are the parents of six children and they live in Rexburg, Idaho, which they love most of the year, except when it is too hot.

Mormon scriptures provide a glimpse of Zion—a godly community of peace, unity, and equality—that is similar to viewing a distant galaxy through a powerful telescope. It is at once both astonishing and inspiring. But it can also appear deeply discomfiting and alien, because the core concepts of that far-off community are so fundamentally different from some of our most cherished earthly traditions. This is especially true when it comes to standards of stewardship and surplus, along with their core orientation of selflessness. These organizing criteria for a Zion community directly challenge free market principles of ownership and acquisition, along with their driving engine of self-interest—cultural forces so strong and pervasive that their gravitational fields become nearly impossible to escape as we desperately stretch towards other stars.

I first began to appreciate the intensity of this tug while still in high school. Sitting on a school bus one afternoon, nursing a youthful and eager hope for Zion, where everyone was "of one heart" and "there was no poor," I contemplated how I might actually live in such a universe.[1] Were there things I could do here and now, or at least in the near future, to help bring that world into being? Gazing out the bus window, I considered for the first time the challenging calculus of stewardship and surplus. How well would I manage the Lord's resources? (I didn't have many resources at the time, but I fully expected some to eventually come my way.) How much of those resources would I honestly require to meet the needs of my future family? What might then be returned to the Lord's storehouse for others to use?

Having little experience in such matters, I nevertheless tried to calculate the needs of my future family. My financially naïve brain settled on what seemed a reasonable number: $30,000. Yes. That was about right. Surely I could support a family on an annual salary of $30,000. And no matter how much my salary might grow (and I assumed at the time that it would eventually grow quite large), I would use only $30,000 and give the rest of it away—to the church, to the poor, to whomever needed it. Excited at the prospect of living a more Zion-like existence, I turned to my seatmate—a good friend, faithful Mormon, and daughter of a successful doctor—and explained my intentions. From her bewildered and almost indignant stare, I knew I had misfired. "Why in the world would you do that?" she asked. "It's your money. You worked for it. You should be able to enjoy it. Why would *anyone* do that?"

That afternoon, discouraged and deflated by her response, I realized for the first time how radically countercultural Zion really is. That conclusion was borne out, both by subsequent conversations with other fellow Mormons, and as I wrestled with my own selfish inclinations. The myth of "ownership" is deeply embedded in Mormon culture, especially its American variants. But some people I admire have managed to resist the myth because they realize that we own *nothing*. Nada. Zilch. Everything belongs to God. "I, the Lord, stretched out the heavens," the divine voice declared to Joseph Smith, "and built the earth, my very handiwork; and all things therein are mine." While the purpose of this creation is "to provide for my saints," He declared, such provision "must needs be done in mine own way."[2] And the Lord's way isn't to give us mortals *any* ownership over *any* part of His creation. Rather God's way is to teach us principles of good stewardship. He is the owner. We are merely the caretakers—and relatively poor ones at that. Gratefully, He seems to be a rather patient schoolmaster and a forgiving landlord.

Thus personal ownership and private property are merely illusions, constructs of a fallen world. Anything we think is "ours" is really just a small portion of God's property for which we *may* have been given minor and temporary responsibility. I say "may" because I am not altogether sure we don't frequently attempt to seize control and assume responsibility over certain portions of the Lord's property when no actual stewardship has been bestowed. Like eager children who discover warm cookies cooling on a kitchen counter, we sometimes mistakenly assume—because they are so easily within our grasp—the treats were made for us, when they were really meant for someone else.

Achieving a mental switch from ownership to stewardship—a switch I have never fully executed—may be one of the most difficult transitions to make. Modern culture is constantly conspiring against us, repeatedly reminding us of our "rights," incessantly encouraging us to savor our "rewards," and constantly whispering in our ears that seductive refrain—"yours, yours, yours." If we somehow manage to resist our culture's gravitational pull and shift to a stewardship orientation, it can completely change the trajectory of our lives.

If the home I live in isn't "mine," for example, if I am merely a steward of someone else's structure, then I have to constantly ask the question, "What does the owner want done with *His* house?" I suspect He would want His house to be available to some of His other children (beyond my immediate relatives, or those who are easy to love and live with) who need shelter and kindness and care. I suspect He would wish it filled with repentance and forgiveness and purity. I suspect He would yearn for truth and integrity and generosity to be both taught and lived by those who dwell in His house.

But in the end it doesn't really matter what I merely suspect. If I am a true and faithful steward, I will constantly consult the Owner regarding His plans and wishes, then listen carefully and execute His instructions. And this spirit of consultation will extend beyond my physical stewardships—houses, cars, clothes, electronics, and bank accounts—to include all of the "things" over which God has given me some responsibility—time, talents, choices, and various emotional and intellectual resources. If I am truly honest with myself, I must confess I don't consult or listen to the Owner regarding His resources nearly as often as I should.

I fall short as well with a necessary corollary to stewardship—the practice of identifying and returning surplus resources. According to a revelation to Joseph Smith known as "The Law of the Church," God declared, "if there shall be properties in the hands of the church, or any individuals of it, more than is necessary for their support . . . it shall be kept to administer to those who have not, from time to time, that every man who has need may be amply supplied and receive according to his wants." This surplus—or "residue"—is to "be kept in my storehouse, to administer to the poor and the needy."[3] And calculating a "residue" was exactly what I was trying to do on that school bus in high school. How much would I need? How much could go back to the Lord's storehouse? Those questions were merely theoretical at the time. I had no resources, no residue—or so I thought. Ten years later I was confronted with the first real test of my convictions—before I had even reached my arbitrary $30,000 threshold, no less—and learned, rather painfully, how quickly we can come to see all "our" resources as "necessary." It's illusory; we all have residue.

The lesson occurred because while I may talk a good game, my wife Dawn is, and has always been, a much better and naturally intuitive practitioner of Zion principles. While we were still in graduate school, with two children, living in her parents' basement, working a part-time job, trying to take preliminary exams and do research, paying off debts—just "scraping by," as the saying goes—Dawn confronted me as I arrived home from work.

"I feel like we should be giving more."

"How much more?" I asked.

"Another ten percent of our income."

I nearly laughed. (Good thing I didn't.)

"How? With what?" I declared more than asked. I was responsible for the budget at the time (she has since taken over), and I knew that every dollar was stretched to the limit. We were lucky to get a date night once in a while, even with free babysitting from her parents. Besides, we were already giving ten percent to the Church in tithing. How could we offer more? "There is no possible way we could give that much."

"Well, just think about it. It's an impression I had today."

I've learned to never discount Dawn's impressions, but to wait for confirmation. Sure enough, later that day as I sat on a street corner watching the bustle of the city, waiting for "my" car to be repaired, the true Owner gently knocked His recalcitrant steward sideways.

"She's right," whispered a soft but firm voice inside my head. "You have more surplus than you think."

Ashamed I hadn't been more receptive to the initial proposal, I went home and apologized to the more open-minded steward, but still swallowed hard as she set the plan in motion.

Not content to simply give more to the Church, Dawn found additional ways to distribute the Lord's surplus. She discovered that a local homeless shelter needed bedding and pillows, and she bought them a nice collection. Seeing a young mother in need of baby clothes, she proceeded to provide. I watched in amazement—at both her extraordinary skill in identifying and meeting needs, and at the minimal effect it had on our budget. She and the Lord were absolutely right—big surprise, I know—we had more surpluses, more "residue," than my small mind had been able to conceive. We never missed those resources. Our family remained fed and clothed and warm. We met all of our obligations. And we even managed a few date nights.

Dawn has since become extremely adept at sniffing out surpluses in our lives. Scouring our closets and gardens and bank accounts, she delights in finding resources to help and lift and bless people. The truly extraordinary thing is how it boomerangs back. Every time she gives something away, something else our family needs seems to drop into our laps—manna from heaven, the Lord redistributing His property to meet the needs and wants of His children. It has almost become a game for her—sniff out the surplus, give it away, wait for the blessings.

This natural Spirit-guided redistribution of wealth and talent gives me hope in the distant galaxy we call Zion, where everyone is "of one heart" and there are "no poor," is actually attainable. Here. Now. In this life. If we truly want it. If we simply embrace stewardship and surplus—and all of their implications—with love and integrity and generosity.

I know it isn't that simple. Not with so many cultural forces pulling us in other directions. I appreciate how difficult the journey toward Zion can be, because I'm nowhere near the forefront, not even in my own family. I'm primarily a spectator, or at most, an enthusiastic booster. My own selfish desires—my sometimes casualness with God's resources, my inattention to the needs of others, and the petty ways I protect "my" time and "my" talents and "my" energy—all speak to how far I have to go before I am ready to join that divine community. But Dawn and others like her continue to inspire me that perhaps I too might obtain the Promised Land. The Spirit of the Owner continues to whisper in my ear, encouraging me to reach beyond myself and join with others to reach for the stars.

NOTES

1. See Moses 7:18, The Pearl of Great Price.
2. Doctrine & Covenants 104:14–16.
3. Doctrine & Covenants 42:33–34.

Building Zion: Apostles and Improv
by Linda Hoffman Kimball

LINDA HOFFMAN KIMBALL earned a BA from Wellesley College and an MFA from Boston University. A convert to the Church of Jesus Christ of Latter-day Saints, she has published several books on topics as wide ranging as the spiritual aspects of food, the challenges of the LDS women's network of Visiting Teaching, and her latest, *Candy Canes & Christmastime: Enhancing the Holidays in the Real World*. She has written a children's picture book *Come with Me on Halloween*. She writes for the Exponent II Journal (with which she has been affiliated since 1974) and is a monthly blogger at Segullah. Linda is also an artist with special interest in printmaking and mixed media.

The first time I went to Zion I got a terrible sunburn on the beach. I was fourteen and had traveled with my mother and sisters from our Chicago suburb to the town of Zion, Illinois, just south of the Wisconsin boarder on beautiful Lake Michigan. Despite the sunburn, my overall memory of the place is positive.

This was before I became a Mormon. A committed Christian from the time I could sing "Jesus Loves Me, This I Know," I heard my Protestant ministers use the word "Zion" in comforting contexts referring to the heavenly Jerusalem in the sweet by-and-by. It was in the name of a lot of cemeteries, too.

When I learned in my freshman year of college that God wanted me to be a Mormon, I heard about Zion as a community of believers living "of one heart and one mind" where evil didn't dwell. This was a noble concept, and, I quickly learned from the eager missionaries, this was generally understood to be Utah.

Certainly it was for the nineteenth-century pioneers. They had fled a hostile country to a place "far away in the west." Theirs *was* a geographical Zion, an isolated land where "no one shall come to hurt or make afraid." It was to be the setting for the experiment in building the Kingdom of God on earth. Eliza R. Snow had cautionary warnings for newcomers. Don't expect any gold paved streets in *that* Zion!

Think not, when you gather to Zion,

Your troubles and trials are through—

That nothing but comfort and pleasure

Are waiting in Zion for you:

No, no; 'tis designed as a furnace,

All substance, all textures to try—

To consume all the "wood, hay and stubble,"

And the gold from the dross purify.[1]

A twentieth-century girl proud of my Prairie State, I wasn't buying into that kind of old-time regionalism. I had a hard time relating to hymns like "Firm as the Mountains Around Us" or "High on a Mountain Top." It was unsettling to learn that a line in W. W. Phelps hymn "Praise to the Man" (written to mourn the death of Joseph Smith at the hands of an angry mob in Carthage, Illinois in 1844) at first read differently than its current iteration. The "blood shed by assassins" that we now understand will "plead unto heaven" was originally invoked to "stain Illinois."

My Protestant heart knew the importance of my individual spiritual life. The concept of a *group* dynamic hadn't really occurred to me. My *Mormon* heart came to understand the gritty task of developing both a personal relationship with Divinity *and* the imperative of working toward unity as a whole body of believers. God's kingdom has no zip code.

Hard as it is to live in the real world—riddled with chaos and crisis as it is—that is what I believe Christ has asked of me. To build Zion—the unity of a spiritually thriving community—is, I believe, my task. Our task.

Mormons tend to see life's ultimate purpose as tied to a verse in the Pearl of Great Price. In the account, where Deity is planning the beginnings of humankind, they announce in Abraham 3:25: "And we shall prove them herewith, to see if they will do all things whatsoever the Lord their God shall command them." I have never particularly felt drawn to that verse. I get an image of grumpy judges with gavels in their hands waiting for me to mess up. I think it encourages fear rather than love. I believe that love—the dynamic kind that chooses holiness—is the hallmark of God. As I said, "Jesus loves me, this I know."

Christ said in Matthew 22:37–39 that "all the law and the prophets" hang on these two commandments, *not* on the particulars of kosher law, cleanliness codes, or the contemporary Latter-day Saint blood sport of defining "modest" clothing.

> Thou shalt love the Lord thy God with all thy heart, and with all thy soul, and with all thy mind. This is the first and great commandment. And the second is like unto it, Thou shalt love thy neighbour as thyself.

That is not to say that I don't keep the LDS requirements exacted of me. I do. And, despite my impatient craving for further light and knowledge in some regards, I consider my responsibilities as a temple ordinance worker to be sacred and something God specifically wants me to do.

There was a time in the early 1980s when I thought maybe I had misread God's directive to align myself with the Mormons. As a convert of just a decade, I happened on an address by a General Authority that troubled me to my core. It provided my first startling lesson on the hard work establishing Zion might entail.

This leader's thesis was that church members were pursuing an "unwise" course in establishing a personal relationship with Jesus Christ. To him it seemed too familiar, not sufficiently reverential. He articulated his views about the specific and precise functions of the Father, Son, and Holy Spirit who, one in purpose and will, make up the Godhead. He even defined what emotions we should attach to each.

His remarks ran counter to everything I knew about my spiritual life before and *after* joining the church. Give up my personal relationship with Christ? That was heretical to me. If being a Mormon required giving that up, I couldn't possibly stay Mormon. What if that apostle was accurately depicting Mormon theology? What had I gotten myself into? Just what did Mormons believe about Jesus anyway? I was troubled and confused.

I decided to read through the Book of Mormon thoroughly this time, with full attention. I underlined every reference to Christ, searching for understanding.

It soon became clear that the focal point of the book would be the appearance of the Savior in the Americas. Everything before it looked forward to that event; everything after it referred back to it. What would He say at this long-awaited event? What would His first words be? How would He distill His message? It was critically important to know. Was there going to be room for me to stay—or would I have to go?

First came the consolation. When I got to 3 Nephi 11, I thrilled at the personal, intimate invitation for each person to come—one by one—to touch the Savior's wounds. Afterward, the people fell at the feet of Jesus and worshipped Him.

Christ "clarifies" His relationship with the other members of the Godhead in a majestic, almost musical canon of witness. He explains that "the Father, and the Son, and the Holy Ghost are one; and I am in the Father, and the Father in me, and the Father and I are one."

At this most crucial juncture in the Nephite timeline and, for that matter, in human history, Jesus feels this "explanation" is clear enough and important enough to repeat it at least three times without further elaboration. This spare, circular, energetic, free flowing "bearing of record" resonated with me. On that particularly sacred occasion God wasn't preoccupied with parsing His/Their identity.

Besides this witness to the unity of the Godhead, Jesus defines His core doctrine. He says:

The father commandeth all men, every where to repent and be
lieve in me; and whoso believeth in me, and is baptized, the same
shall be saved. . . . Ye must repent and become as a child, and be
baptized in my name, or ye can in nowise receive these things.

He repeats it again, in case we missed it the first two times. Then, to
bring the point home to people who have just experienced tempests,
winds, floods, and shifting foundations, He adds:

Whoso shall declare more or less than this, and establish it for my
doctrine . . . buildeth upon a sandy foundation, and the gates of
hell standeth open to receive such when the floods come and the
winds beat upon them.[2]

I found Jesus' distilled declaration of doctrine a relief. In this central
story of the Book of Mormon was the heart of the Gospel message.

The caution about affirming "more or less than this" was satisfying,
too. I don't understand the approach of that apostle who disturbed me
so. I find the obsessive hunt for theological precision futile and in
the end spiritually unproductive if not worse, since Jesus describes
it as tempting the gates of hell. I recall Joseph Smith's response to the
censure of a man for teaching "incorrect doctrine." He said:

I do not like the old man being called up for erring in doctrine.
It looks too much like the Methodists, and not like the Latter-
day Saints. Methodists have creeds which a man must believe or
be asked out of their Church. I want the liberty of thinking and
believing as I please. It feels so good not to be trammeled.[3]

Then came the wallop. 3 Nephi 11 gave the challenging lesson that puts
real muscle into the group dynamic aspect of the Gospel, the exercise
of establishing Zion. By coming to Christ as a little child, I agree to
take Christ's (incredibly hard) challenge in 3 Nephi 11:28–30, and avoid
"disputations . . . concerning the points of my doctrine" and "the spirit
of contention." "Such things should be done away," Jesus insisted.

How that's supposed to happen isn't articulated. It staggered me
to realize there needs to be room in the church for both me *and* the

troubling apostle. And on top of all that, I was to love him, too!

It doesn't mean I will ever persuade that apostle to share my views, nor will I be converted to his. We won't have "unity" in that way. There will be no mind meld. But somehow—and this is where the challenges is so, um, exciting—I have to learn to make room for those whose approach is different from mine—for those whose brains and hearts crave the concrete and defined where mine feasts on paradox and koan. I would like to think he, and others who share his approach, understand that there is room for me, too. It doesn't always feel like it, but that has no bearing on my responsibility to make this church a place of peace and welcome for all who love God.

My reading of 3 Nephi 11 during those anxious days tethered me to this Mormon place, gave me a greater clarity on what creating Zion has to include and continues to give my spiritual aerobic system a robust workout.

Another example of learning the Gospel's group dynamics came through a secular opportunity I had to watch playwright and director Mary Zimmerman demonstrate at Chicago's Goodman Theater how she selects a cast for her brilliant productions. She rarely has a script before she casts a play. She thrives on collaboration with her cast as she develops it so selection of a cast is a crucial task. She's not Mormon and had no plan to provide a deep spiritual lesson, but it worked on me that way, anyway.

For this demonstration she played improvisational theater games with a group of about twenty actors. One of the games involved a prop. I think this time it was a (now old-fashioned) curly corded princess telephone. The game was called (I think) "This is not a . . .". She started with the prop and said "This is not a telephone; this is a . . ." and then she called it something imaginative like (though it surely wasn't this) "a matador's hat with a built-in moustache!" acting it out to the delight of all. Then someone else in the circle grabbed it and said "This is not a matador's hat with a built-in moustache; it is a . . . jump rope!" and around the circle it would go, one clever transformation after another.

When the game was over, Ms. Zimmerman shared why she used that game to help select a cast. She hadn't let the actors in on her strategy. They thought they were just playing an improv game to goose creativity and imagination. While the actors laughed and grabbed and pretended with the prop, she was observing each of them ("proving them herewith"). Yes, she looked for creativity. But it also gave her a way to intuit the group dynamics. She identified the reticent and the show-offs and the ones who seemed busy in their own heads trying to think of the "best" response to get the biggest laugh. She sussed out the ones who were more concerned about their own wittiness rather than the ensemble experience. The ones she selected were the ones who were extremely imaginative but also invested in the group as a whole.

Instead of selecting the "standouts" from the group, the director was on the hunt for those who could make the group as a *unit* be both brilliant and cohesive—and enjoy the process.

That for me is the process of establishing Zion. It's keeping in mind that there is something holy and necessary to nourishing my individual spiritual relationship with God and at the same time committing to value, make room for, and build cohesion among the body of believers. I can't say I necessarily enjoy the process. It's sometimes excruciating work. Obviously it wasn't all fun and games for Jesus either. But I belong to Him, and Christ has called me to it. "This is not a . . ." doomed enterprise; this is a bidding from my Savior.

NOTES

1. *Sacred Hymns and Spiritual Songs for the Church of Jesus Christ of Latter-Day Saints* (Salt Lake City: Deseret Book, 20th ed., 1891), 393.

2. 3 Nephi 11:32, 37–39, Book of Mormon.

3. B. H. Roberts, *A Comprehensive History of the Church of Jesus Christ of Latter-day Saints,* 6 vols. (Salt Lake City: Deseret Book, 1930), 5:340.

Of Sinners and Saints:
Zion and the LGBT Contingent
by Josh Weed

JOSH WEED is a licensed marriage and family therapist residing in Washington State, where he and his wife, Lolly, parent their four daughters. Josh's writing has appeared in *The Washington Post, Dialogue: A Journal of Mormon Thought*, and the Mormon Church's *Deseret News*. His coming-out post went viral in 2012 and he has been featured prominently on TV, radio and on various websites. He maintains a blog at joshweed.com.

One Sunday, I attended an LDS sacrament meeting unlike any LDS Church meeting I have ever attended. It was in the University District of Seattle very near Capitol Hill, where there is a very large gay community. I heard about this meeting when I received a flyer reaching out to the local congregants. (I live in a suburb forty-five minutes south of Seattle and belong to a different congregation.) The flyer invited gay and lesbian Mormons to come to a special Sacrament meeting. The flyer said amazing things—things I'm sure the gay members of the church are unaccustomed to seeing. The flyer said gay members were needed and wanted. It said that they would be welcomed as a part of the "ward family"—as an integral part of the congregation. It said if they came, they would be *safe*.

My wife and I knew we needed to attend this meeting. I am a gay man, but a gay man who has chosen to be married to a woman. As such, I am a fervent supporter of my gay brothers and sisters within the Mormon faith—even those whose paths look very different from my own. The two of us and our three young, energetic daughters arrived late to the meeting and sat down—like a small tornado—in a pew just as the first talk ended. We got the girls settled, took a deep breath, and it finally hit me what was happening at the pulpit. A woman named Celeste was speaking. She had visible tattoos on both arms and short blonde hair, spiked upward. She was tearing up. She was saying she had been asked to speak on what it is like for her to be a gay member of the Mormon Church. She was standing at the pulpit saying words like "lesbian" and "coming out" and we were *in sacrament meeting*. Her face radiated the spirit of Jesus Christ as she spoke eloquently about her journey—about not fitting, about feeling rejected, about feeling anger that *this* was happening to her, even though she loved the church and wanted to be a part of it.

I could hardly believe what I was hearing. Before publicly coming out in 2012, my memories of the discussion of homosexuality in the Mormon Church were not pleasant. I remember guys in my apartment, while attending a Mormon University, talking about how if they had a gay roommate they would "beat the crap out of him." I sat silently. I *was* their roommate. I *was* gay. I remember multiple lessons in priesthood meetings in which "the gays" were blamed for the degradation of society and were labeled deviants. I remember lessons in which members of the church bemoaned the sad state of affairs we live in—a world in which gay people *exist*. Surely the end of times is near—gay people want to *marry each other*. I heard things like "Satan has really got a hold of this world" or "our society is *worse* than Sodom and Gomorrah!" or "these people just want attention, with their parades and their promiscuous lifestyles. They are perverts." I remember other harsh words being used, by local leaders and prophets alike, to describe both the acts of homosexuality as well as the people who enacted them. Words like "abominable" and "detestable" and "crime against nature" and "unnatural and wrong." I would sit silently while these comments were made, wishing I could speak out, wishing I could say "I am *one* of these people. You are talking about *real people*."

At the time, to say such a thing was unheard of. For most of my life, I knew of zero "out" gay Mormons who were still active in the church. To "out" myself didn't feel like a real option. There was very little information from any level of the church, and what was written was often woefully inaccurate (claiming gayness could be cured, or was a plight that was largely self-inflicted through sin.) Even when I contemplated coming out as a gay man married to a woman two years ago, some of my church leaders encouraged me not to do so. "Isn't that the kind of thing that's best left private?" I was asked. One leader in particular tried to drive home the point. "But Josh," he explained, "if there were a *heterosexual* man who liked to have sex with a lot of women, it would be inappropriate for him to share that struggle—so it's also inappropriate for you to share yours." I was so baffled by this comparison I hardly had a response. As a therapist specializing in sexual addiction, I observe there are few things *healthier* than to have people who struggle with compulsive sexual behavior talk more openly—and feel less shame—about it. How does my coming out as a gay man even remotely resemble a straight man wanting to have sex with many women? Couldn't that be said of *many* straight men?

In recent years, though, I've seen amazing changes, and those changes make my hope for a Zion in which our gay brothers and sisters feel that being welcomed is more and more possible. I've seen men and women share their sexual orientation with their friends and families and wards amidst an outpouring of support, both on-line and in person. I've participated in conferences and talks where gay and lesbian Mormons speak their truth and receive love and understanding. I've witnessed firesides and other meetings where church members can ask questions they've long wondered about the experience of being homosexual, and can hear those questions answered by their LGBT brothers and sisters. I've seen dialogue and I've seen growth. I've seen people's knowledge base increase because of the church's website, mormonsandgays.org, and I have personally been touched by that website's wonderful instructions regarding loving gay people.

But until that Sunday, I'd never seen *anything* like this.

I'd never seen a sacrament meeting that would be warm and loving to a gay person with his or her partner. I'd never heard a talk about homosexuality by a homosexual person. I'd never seen a chapel turn into a haven where men and women who wanted to remain a part of the church (even peripherally, and even if they were living a non-hetero-normative lifestyle) would feel *safe*.

And yet, there I was, hearing this talk by Celeste. I listened to her in amazement as she told about a time she was feeling anger. She was struggling with feeling the pain of rejection within her church. She explained she was feeling hurt and lonely. She told of how, during this sensitive time, someone asked a very hurtful question—a question that should never be asked of any Mormon person who has a doubt, or feels anger, or is challenged by a doctrine. It is a question that many gay Mormons are asked as they grapple with their identity within the church, and a question that divides us. It is a question that wounds. It is a question that doesn't belong in Zion: "Why don't you just leave?"

I began to tear up. As she spoke, I had become aware of my surroundings, and of the people I personally knew in the congregation around me. My mind lighted on them: the former Relief Society President sitting a few rows back who had recently, after decades of loneliness and poor mental health as a lesbian in the church, fallen in love and partnered with a woman, and was now trying desperately to find a place in her church; the elderly gay man who had recently, after years of agonizing contemplation, decided to leave his wife because he finally realized the promises made to him by his leaders that his sexual orientation would change after marriage had been unfounded; the younger gay man, in his twenties, trying to decide if he was *actually* going to commit to live a life of celibacy in order to remain temple-worthy. These were just the people I happened to know—also present were countless other LGBT Mormons. These people had come to sacrament meeting to be fed. They had come to be given fuel fit for their situation, and each of them had every reason to ask him or herself the same question. "If it's so hard, if it's so complicated, if it's so painful, and if people can sometimes be so cruel, why stay? Why don't I just leave?"

My heart swelled as Celeste continued her story. The answer she gave to that question was so simple but also so profound. "Because," she said, "*I don't want to.*" In that moment, she says, she realized that she didn't *want* to leave. She is gay and she is Mormon. She is both. And she didn't want alter either of those parts of her identity.

The gay people I happened to knew in the congregation, and the many others I had never met, were at this meeting because they *don't want to leave.* They don't want to be rejected. They don't want to be excluded. They want to congregate with the Saints, even in the midst of their complicated decisions and, at times, heart-rending feelings, and they want to hear the word of God. They want to sing the hymns of their youth and they want to rejoice in the spirit they feel as they listen to the prayers and the talks. They want to hear about the restoration, and they want to hear about Jesus Christ. They want to give talks like Celeste was giving a talk, and they want to participate, and they want to add their gifts. They want to play the piano and they want to sing and they want to hug their friends. They want to come closer to Christ, and they want to watch the sacrament trays of bread and water passed by deacons, and they want to listen to the testimonies of their brothers and sisters in the gospel. They want to be strengthened, and they want to give strength. They want to be loved by their people, and they want to love their people.

They don't "just leave" because *they don't want to leave.*

Zion, in its truest form, needs us all. That is my vision of the future—a Zion in which each LGBT Mormon feels safe to worship, no matter where in their life path they find themselves. We must ensure Zion is a safe and welcoming place—not just for those who look, sound, and appear to fit Mormonism as we know and understand it, but for *all* of God's children. Zion needs to be a safe haven for everyone; the downtrodden and the worried, the doubtful and the hurt, the sinners *and* the saints. For, indeed, each saint among us is a sinner, and each sinner a *latter-day saint.*

I Have Found the Piece which I Had Lost

by Kate Kelly

KATE KELLY is a zealous advocate, passionate activist, and lifelong Mormon. She has a JD from American University Washington College of Law, the only law school in the world founded by, and for, women. She is currently living and working in Nairobi, Kenya litigating before the African Commission on Human and Peoples' Rights. In 2013 she founded a group called Ordain Women to advocate for gender equality in the Mormon Church. She was excommunicated from the church in June 2014 for speaking out against the fundamental exclusion of women, but her work for parity in religion continues unabated. You can find out more about Kate at katekellyesq.com.

*And when she hath found it, she calleth her friends and her neighbours together, saying, Rejoice with me; for I have found the piece which I had lost. –*LUKE 15:9[1]

I grew up as the oldest of four siblings in a Mormon home. My parents, both converts, raised us in the church. In many ways we were a very typical LDS family. We went to church every Sunday. We participated in road shows. We hosted the missionaries for dinner. We reenacted the pioneer trek where we built a wooden handcart ourselves and trekked around in the mountains in old-timey clothes pretending we were pioneers coming across the plains. I was baptized when I was eight years old, by my dad.

Growing up I was the classic domineering oldest sibling. One day, when I was five, and my little sister was three, I ordered her to eat her dinner by saying, "Just do it and be done!" She complied, and so began my career as an assertive person. In spite of—or perhaps because of?—the myriad problems all families face, I had a relatively normal Mormon upbringing.

When I was eighteen, my mom sat me down and said, "I want you to know you have an older sister I never told you about." It was a rude awakening; up to that point I had imagined we were just about the most idyllic Mormon family imaginable. In spite of my normal dosage of teen angst, I did not see my parents as flawed individuals—I saw them as near-perfect.

As my mother went on to tell this excruciating story, long buried in her past, she sobbed uncontrollably. I was utterly stunned; prior to this, I had only seen her "Sunday tears" in sacrament meeting when she was bearing her testimony. I had never witnessed such sorrow and pain in her, never seen her so achingly weep. I sat mute and sullen, trying to process my own emotions over these revelations as they unfolded from her between deep gasping breaths.

I learned my mom had been pregnant as a fifteen-year-old and had relinquished the child to a closed adoption. The adoptive father was a surgeon at the hospital where my mother had given birth, and he had saved a copy of the original birth certificate and other documents related to her identity and gave them to my sister when she reached adulthood. Because of his forethought and kindness, my sister was able to locate our mother in her early twenties, and they began the process of meeting and reconnecting. At first my mom was dazed because she knew nothing about my sister and hadn't imagined she would ever see her again. She had never spoken to any of us about a sister, about her lost child. My sister's existence had been kept a secret from everyone, and my mother had to navigate new waters with a new daughter, as well as with her other children. After several years of privately nurturing this new relationship with her previously lost child, my mom finally felt comfortable and ready for all of us to meet her first daughter, Anne.

As the previously-eldest, my mom told me first. I imagine few things more shocking than finding out you have a sibling you never knew. It was a reality-altering experience, one of those out-of-body moments, but instead of watching yourself you are watching an after-school-special. The news was so biologically matter-of-fact that it felt all at once dramatic and mundane.

To be charitable to my eighteen-year-old self, I'll admit I was "predictably resistant" to the idea that I was no longer the oldest and I had a new, adult sibling to integrate into my worldview. She was a stranger to me and my siblings, and we struggled with feelings of dealing with the past. Would this put a tarnish on our Mormon street cred, admitting our family had a child out of wedlock? It seems selfish in retrospect, but social dynamic and expectation are strong pressures in Mormonism.

Though I resisted change initially, life moved on and took me with it. Through patience, kindness, and a willingness to love on all of our parts, my mother's daughter Anne became a cherished part of our extended family. She came on vacation with us to Hawaii, and we wore leis made out of orchids and tasted her vegetarian cooking. She came with us to church, despite not being raised Mormon, and we introduced her as my mother's "friend" from Connecticut. This was a hilarious family joke, as the family resemblance between my mother and Anne is astounding. My mom made my sister Amy and me learn a special musical number for the day Anne came to church for the first time, to make her feel welcome:

> Dear to the heart of the Shepherd,
> Dear are the sheep of his fold;
> Dear is the love that he gives them,
> Dearer than silver or gold.
> Dear to the heart of the Shepherd,
> Dear are his "other" lost sheep;
> Over the mountains he follows,
> Over the waters so deep.

We are still a messy, imperfect unit, as all families are. But we are a better, and a more whole family, now that Anne is home. Anne has a daughter of her own now, named Lily. My husband Neil and I are Lily's godparents. We enjoy Christmases and holidays together. My mom and Anne both love to cook and we join them in the kitchen as sous-chefs. Anne joined us for the Ordain Women priesthood action, and shared in what can only be described as a sisterly solidary with our sorrow and grief at being excluded from our place of worship because we are women. It is as if we missed her all along in life, but we never knew it. With her as part of our family, our unrealistic Mormon ideal-family image is gone, but we are magnificently more whole.

. . if ye have experienced a change of heart, and if ye have felt to sing the song of redeeming love, I would ask, can ye feel so now? –ALMA 5:26

When I was a missionary for the church, there was one particularly lively and gung-ho sister missionary from Springville, Utah in my training group. This sister was one of those so-eager-she-plasters-inspirational-quotes-everywhere-and-sweats-enthusiasm type of missionary. Her genuine excitement was disarming to anyone more reserved. One of the quotes she spread with her typical proselyting zeal, and which, despite my dislike for platitudes, effected me deeply, was "Change, don't stay the same. But, be consistent in living gospel principles."

It was as Hermana Kelly, serving a mission in Barcelona, Spain where I came to see the gospel as a gospel of change. As a missionary you are uniquely situated to be closely involved in sensitive issues in the lives of near strangers. People invite you to their homes to discuss God, their loves, their struggles, their addictions, and everything in between. As missionaries, we see the most intimate portraits of the daily lives of people. I had the privilege of bearing witness to monumental change in the lives of many. I helped a widow suffering crippling loneliness. I supported a woman struggling with life-threatening bulimia. I befriended a woman besieged by severe mental illness and delusion. I counseled couples on the verge of marital dissolution. I experienced tremendous vulnerability and beheld a willingness to change on the part of many people. People can and do change their minds. They changed their hearts. Witnessing this change changed me.

As a people, we cannot become of "one heart and one mind" if we each stay in our own individual, comfortable camps of thought. We must achieve, at the bare minimum, mutual respect and understanding.

We often have to leave the comfort and familiarity of old patterns, old habits, and old paradigms. We must pass through discomfort in order to make it to a new place.

One of my all time favorite photographs is a postcard I bought in Portland, Oregon. It is shot from behind and shows a man moving forward across a desert. In his hands a large flag is unfurled. It reads, red letters on white cloth, "I have changed my mind." The most magnificent and Christ-like people I know all have one common characteristic: they are willing to change their minds. They are willing to bend, almost to the point of breaking, in order to find happiness and greater understanding. They are willing to change.

And the Lord called his people Zion, because they were of one heart and one mind, and dwelt in righteousness; and there was no poor among them. –MOSES 7:18

This is one of the most central questions for twenty-first-century Mormonism: Is the gospel, as practiced by my church, an open, inclusive place for all of God's children? Like my family and our lost sister, Mormons are missing out by marginalizing people—people of color, women, and our LGTBQIA brothers and sisters.

When something is missing, sometimes you don't even realize it until it reappears. The transition can be tumultuous, but reconciliation and acceptance are beautiful, healing balms. When I hear people say various iterations of "it can't be that way because it hasn't been that way in the past," they are clinging to the stability they think intransigence provides. They are not welcoming the change of heart required of each of us through the Gospel of Christ. As I learned to accept a sibling who is part of me and was part of a messy past and difficult to reconcile with my current worldview, I grew as a person and as a saint.

I think of my family, and what tremendous joy and love we have found in accepting and in even *welcoming* change. Zion means to me working through the messy, painful imperfections we have as individuals and as a Church. The transition to become a Zion people is not about the fantastical transformations of a fairy godmother. Zion cannot be facilitated with the wave of a magic wand. It is at times a difficult, arduous slog. Accepting new information, people, and paradigms is hard work. As a people, however, we cannot reach a state where we are of "one heart and one mind" by avoiding struggle, dialogue, and conversion. On my mission, I taught people the struggle is worth the reward. I have since come to understand the struggle is it. The struggle is Zion.

As a people we need to find what we are missing, even if we are not currently cognizant of the absence. The first step is conceding that we might be missing something at all. Zion requires us to adapt, to constantly reexamine old solidified notions. An institution that sends two eighteen-year-olds into homes around the world and asks people point-blank to give up everything they thought they were before must certainly foster the same dynamic flexibility of those already in the fold. Change isn't always—or ever—easy. But being willing to change is the beginning of the required opening of our hearts and the turning of our spirits to face in the direction of God.

As I learned at age eighteen, sometimes change will move along taking you with it. Embracing transformation and newness stretches us. Accepting Anne made me grow. It is now incumbent on the church to make way for a new Zion where all are equal. In spite of difficulty, there is beauty to be found in the process. And, a resplendent heavenly family where all are welcome will be the reward.

Lucy Mack Smith, the mother of Mormonism's founding prophet, said, "We must cherish one another, watch over one another, comfort one another and gain instruction that we may all sit down in heaven together."[2] Zion is recognizing and embracing the parts of ourselves that are the hardest to see. In the end, we will all rejoice when we have found the piece that we have lost and we can all sit down, as one in Zion, together.

NOTES

1. The scriptures cited in this paper are from the New Testament and the Book of Mormon.

2. Relief Society Minutes, Mar. 24, 1842, Archives of The Church of Jesus Christ of Latter-day Saints, 18–19.

Let Them Eat Cake

by W. Paul Reeve

W. PAUL REEVE is Associate Professor and the Director of Graduate Studies in the History Department at the University of Utah where he teaches courses on Utah history, Mormon history, and the history of the U.S. West. His most recent book, *Religion of a Different Color: Race and the Mormon Struggle for Whiteness*, was published by Oxford University Press. He is also the author of *Making Space on the Western Frontier: Mormons, Miners, and Southern Paiutes*, and co-editor with Ardis E. Parshall of *Mormonism: A Historical Encyclopedia*. With Michael Van Wagenen he co-edited *Between Pulpit and Pew: The Supernatural World in Mormon History and Folklore*. He is the recipient of the University of Utah's Early Career Teaching Award and of the College of Humanities Ramona W. Cannon Award for Teaching Excellence in the Humanities.

Community has always been more important than the individual in Mormonism. Mormonism, in fact, stands as a rejection of life as a Darwinian struggle of all against all, and a refutation of a "survival of the fittest" mentality. Jesus Christ cared for the "unfit" and desired their success. As his disciples in the twenty-first century, Latter-day Saints attempt, always imperfectly, to follow his lead. It is one aspect of my chosen faith I find deeply satisfying and spiritually compelling.

At my baptism when I was eight years old I covenanted to bear one another's burdens that they might be light and to comfort those who stand in need of comfort. As a naïve eight-year-old, I didn't fully understand what I signed up for when I made that covenant. As an adult, learning the global reach of that covenant does not cause me to want to shrink or abandon my promises; rather it fills me with compassion and a desire to leave the world a better place.

I grew up in a home that put these principles into action, so much so that I did not fully understand that there were more selfish philosophies upon which one might organize a worldview. Service and care for those who are less fortunate have been a part of my Christian path from the beginning. My dad was a cattle rancher and my mom was a strong believer in the principle that "charity never faileth." My parents frequently used their resources for the good of others. Each Christmas they had a steer killed and packaged into frozen hamburger, steaks, and roasts. My mom would drive my brother and me to a designated house where it was our job to leave large heavy boxes of beef on the porch, ring the doorbell, and then run for cover. The natural joy of doing something good was always multiplied by the thrill of not getting caught. At the time, the experience was more about the fun of parent-condoned "doorbell ditching" than any moral obligation to the less fortunate. In hindsight, I realize my parents were also teaching me that any society is only as strong as its most vulnerable members and that promising to follow Jesus included a promise to *give* his grace as well as to receive it.

These ideals are not unique to Mormonism, but Mormonism offers a plethora of opportunities to put these ideals into practice. In addition to a lay ministry that offers opportunities for all members of a congregation to serve in "callings," the LDS welfare system also creates additional opportunities to give of oneself. Whenever there was a request for volunteers to work at the LDS peach orchard near my childhood home, I knew my dad would sign up. I recall pruning peach trees, thinning peaches, picking peaches, and canning peaches as yearly occurrences, projects as much a part of being Mormon for me as going to Sunday services. I do not recall finding any broader meaning in the work when I was young. It was mostly about getting the job done so that I could then do what I wanted to do. As an adult, however, I find much deeper purpose in this work. I still volunteer for assignments when opportunities present themselves. It has consequence to me. Some of my most satisfying experiences as a Latter-day Saint have come in the act of canning green beans or beef stew or packaging beans and granola. In fulfilling these assignments I have worked alongside medical doctors, investors, school teachers, bankers, stay-at-home moms, cable installers, businesspeople, lawyers, and others—all people who have given up a portion of their day to work on a LDS Church-owned assembly line to can and package food which they will not personally eat. It is a wonderful feeling when volunteers can do so much to help alleviate hunger and ensure that those who are struggling have sufficient food. Working on an assembly line is both a welcome change of pace from my office job and a needed reminder that I am fortunate to have an office job. It also prompts an easily neglected appreciation for laborers across the globe who hide behind each of my far too convenient purchases at my local grocery store. Most importantly, working on an assembly line spiritually connects me to people who may have fallen on hard times and need assistance to get back on their feet. I always leave these volunteer opportunities tired but fulfilled, happy to give my labor to lift another person in need.

When I heard about Family Humanitarian Expedition, an organization started and run by Latter-day Saints who desire to mitigate the effects of poverty on third world populations, it seemed like a natural outgrowth of the ethos with which I was so familiar. Two people in my LDS congregation, Steve and Rachel von Niederhausern, are leaders in the organization and are models of Christian charity. They are examples of people who see beyond themselves to care for others. Steve and Rachel have been to the remote Polochic region of Guatemala several times to establish relationships with village leaders and to work on various humanitarian projects: building schools, organizing dental and medical clinics, conducting agricultural training, installing stoves, and a variety of other construction projects. During the summer of 2014, my sixteen-year-old son and I joined one such expedition. We slept in sleeping bags, lived without running water and with limited electricity and less than ideal bathroom facilities, including the coldest water for showers I have yet to encounter. We painted a school, helped in a dental clinic, taught health and nutrition classes, played with village kids, mixed concrete for a new floor at a medical clinic, and worked hard at manual labor. It was one of the most fulfilling experiences I have ever shared with my son.

My time in Guatemala and with the people I met there have given me a lot to ponder, things that I imagine I will continue to think about for the rest of my life. What is my place in the vast universe? What is my obligation to my family, friends, neighbors, and strangers whom I have never met? What chance do I have in changing even a small corner of the world? How can I possibly make a difference? I am only one person and the depth of world poverty is staggering.

Doing nothing, however, does not feel like a viable option.

I saw so many examples of God's hands at work over the course of our week in Guatemala. At the end of our week I was exhausted, tired of beans and tortillas for breakfast, and wanting a hot shower, soft bed, and a pleasant bathroom. I was ready to return home to the comforts of life I take for granted every day. I came home and had to remind myself it was okay to drink the water that came out of the tap. I slept for ten hours in a soft bed and took a very long hot shower.

In thinking back over my experience, I can't escape the fact that I left a part of my heart in Guatemala. It is something difficult to articulate. If I didn't go to Guatemala, someone would have taught the health and nutrition classes, painted the school, mixed the concrete at the medical clinic, and sterilized the instruments at the dental clinic. I had no special skills that were required in Guatemala. I represented cheap manual labor. My presence was not crucial or even necessary. I did nothing remarkable, yet why did my experience so completely capture my heart?

Maybe it is because I left feeling more closely knit together in the bonds of affection with the people I served and with whom I served. Maybe it is because I believe that education and basic health care shouldn't be luxuries for the rich and if I can wield a shovel, a paint brush, or rubber gloves in bringing those luxuries to someone who might not have them otherwise, then I feel deeply fulfilled. Maybe it is because I have hope in humanity and hope in Jesus Christ that in lifting a paint roller I might lift a brother and sister whom I've never met into self-sufficiency and a brighter future. Maybe it is because I believe everyone deserves an infant and female wing of their medical clinic, and that it should have a concrete floor. Maybe it is because I believe that my brothers and sisters in Guatemala with bright eyes and happy faces shouldn't have to suffer with painful toothaches. Maybe it is because their bright eyes and happy faces made me forget my first world problems for a week and allowed me to focus on third world problems with practical solutions. Ultimately, I hope it is because in my heart of hearts I love Jesus Christ and in taking up His cross I take up the cross of the poor and needy. We don't have to go to Guatemala to care for the poor and needy; if we covenant to follow Christ, however, we do have to care for the poor and needy. The Lord promises, "He that giveth unto the poor shall not lack."[1] My week in Guatemala is a week in which I lacked running water, warm showers, sanitary bathroom facilities, a soft bed, air conditioning, electricity, clean clothes, cell phone connections, e-mail, Facebook, and TV, and yet it was a week in which I did not lack.

Back in the United States a few months later, a clipboard requesting volunteers to work at the Church's dry pack welfare factory circulated in my congregation one Sunday. I scrawled my name and took note of the date. When I showed up on the assigned day I was somewhat (pleasantly) surprised to learn that we would be packaging chocolate cake mix. My previous experiences as a volunteer included canning healthy and hearty foods which provided nutrition and sustained life, but who decided that chocolate cake mix was a welfare necessity?

As the shift began and I took my place at the quality control station at the head of the conveyor belt, my mind was opened. I imagined moms and dads on assistance struggling to make ends meet with children to feed and clothe—and birthday parties to throw. I imagined a profound sense of relief coming over a mom in such a situation as she went to a LDS welfare store and found packages of chocolate cake mix lining the shelf and available without cost. A child's birthday wish was justification enough for me.

I wondered if there had been some conversation somewhere up the bureaucratic chain of command with some ranking welfare committee deliberating over what products to produce. Was there a discussion on chocolate cake? Was it a welfare necessity? Should the church invest its time, money, and volunteer hours in producing such a commodity? I imagined a scenario that might have played out as such a hypothetical discussion unfolded. Somewhere someone with enough clout to matter must have also thought about birthday parties and moms and dads and the pressures of struggling toward self-sufficiency. Maybe that someone even recalled Isaiah's admonition to not "grind the faces of the poor" or Jesus's reminder that when you have "done it unto one of the least of these my brethren, ye have done it unto me."[2] Maybe it was the Book of Mormon rejoinder that "when ye are in the service of your fellow beings ye are only in the service of your God" that entered that person's mind.[3] Whatever it might have been, I imagined that leader concluding the discussion with a wry smile and settling the matter with a proclamation, "Let them eat cake."

I left my assignment that day with my clothes dusted in cake mix and my spirit lifted. I felt fulfilled yet again to place an unseen and unknown community above my all too selfish heart and content yet again to be Mormon.

NOTES

1. See Proverbs 28: 27.

2. See Isaiah 3: 14–15. The term "grind" refers in this instance to not oppress and humiliate the poor; to not grind their faces in their poverty. See also Matthew 25:40.

3. See Mosiah 2:17, The Book of Mormon.

October
by C. Jane Kendrick

C. JANE KENDRICK is a writer, blogger, columnist, speaker, and community activist. For eight years she has cultivated her award-winning blog CJaneKendrick.com where she writes about life, religion, birthing, wifehood, motherhood, womanhood, body acceptance, her love of community and all the spaces in between. She has also written for the *Deseret News*, *The Arizona Republic*, Segullah and published a book of her essays called *C. Jane Enjoy It!* She lives in Provo, Utah with her husband Christopher, four young children, and a spectacular view of the Wasatch Front.

October's depression came right in on time this year. Like a heavy, black train into a station, it steamed forward, hissed, and grounded right into my chest. It heralds the loss of light in this hemisphere—a darkening of days and a shorter daily time period to work. I grieve the sun on my face and it hurts my heart.

Only, this year it came with a fierce infusion of postpartum inconsistency. Like a whipped center into a baked good, hormones stuffed into my body with no apparent exit. This year, more than ever, I went crazy.

Insomnia and worry danced in my head. I was anxious, uncomfortable, and tired. There were days I'd beg to hibernate, retreat to the bed with arms and legs unfolded wide like I could sleep and stretch the gloom out of me. There was never enough rest.

My personal relationships suffered. Sensitivity took over my balance and I was tipsy and wary and full of second guesses. I was certain I didn't deserve people anyway, I didn't deserve anything. I couldn't be grateful for what was in my world because guilt was in the way. And even though it was always rattling around in my throat, on the verge in my eyes, I couldn't cry because I didn't deserve that either. There was no release.

"Do you want to go see someone?" Christopher asked one morning when the depression had hovered over me all night.

I was too shocked to answer. It bowled me down. I couldn't think or deliver form or function. I was just breathing in and out, in and out. My thoughts couldn't get past the ringing chorus, *you aren't good enough, you've never been good enough, you will never be good enough.*

"Maybe we should get some meds?" he asked again.

On that morning a new limb to my walking dreariness was born, the appendage about hurting others with my hurt. I was about to stop walking and beg to be carried. It was a heavy load for my husband, but he was all I wanted.

I hadn't asked for antidepressants since college, even though I always felt a little seasonal despondency. Medication made the depression go away but it also made me numb, I missed the nuance of emotion. I recognized it as a blessing in pill form, but I decided to use it sparingly. For me, it was a last resort.

"I am going to start a morning meditation routine," I answered. Some tiny part of me knew that the loss of love I felt in my life could be rescued with a heavy dose of consistent, spiritual enlightening. Fear vanished when learning commenced. For me, it has always been my true rescue.

So I started. Every day I'd ignore any impulse to sulk the awakening of my eyes. I prayed, read scriptures and self-help books, and wrote down any good thoughts that bubbled into my head. Every day I asked my Heavenly Father for a little bit of knowledge that I didn't have before. And it came. Tiny bits of ideas, pieces of truth until one morning I was healed. It was a flash of brilliance, and my puzzle was solved. It was this:

There is faith, hope, and charity.

There is past, future, and present.

Faith is believing that everything in my past has a purpose. Every misjudgment, jealousy, and hurt. Every joy, indulgence, and success. All my wrong choices, all my right choices pushed me forward to right now. My rejoicing, my repentance, my realignments, all of it, has brought me here. Faith is believing I have been on an upward progression all my life, guided by the very angels of heaven. There have been no mistakes so grave, no depression so dark, no wind so strong that I've been knocked off course. Faith is believing the past has accumulated for my good. And though it still makes up my soul, the past is over.

Hope is believing the future will come. A future of better things, stronger convictions and securer sense of self. It is having the confidence that everything I don't have today, everything I want, will come because I am worthy of it. Hope says, *I am weak today, but tomorrow I will be a little bit stronger.* Hope can promise all the hurt, all the fear, the anxiety, the lacking, will slowly leave, vanish, and melt away. Hope is okay with the fact that today isn't perfect. Hope holds all the mysteries yet to unfold. Hope is never-ending because the future is always ahead.

Charity is all we have in the present. Our past is gone, our future is yet to be and there is no sense or possibility of really living in either of those two spaces. We remember, we project, but for now, we love. We love all that we have presently, all that our eyes can see and our bodies can touch. We love the people who are in our rooms, in our spaces, in our dreams. We love with intelligence and understanding. We may not have the money we want, the body we crave, the things occupying our desires, but we can love the salary we do make, the body we do have, and the things that fulfill our needs. We love the meals we eat, the shoes we wear, the woman at the grocery store. Charity is the "now" we actually own, the present we can actually manipulate. It's all we have and it's all we have to give.

So be kind to yourself, I heard the Spirit say to me at the end of this watershed moment.

And I've been trying.

Since then, the train in my chest huffed and puffed and is finally pulling off into the distance.

Zion, Sacrifice, Consecration
by Adam S. Miller

ADAM S. MILLER is a professor of philosophy at Collin College in McKinney, Texas. He earned his MA and PhD in philosophy from Villanova University as well as a BA in Comparative Literature from Brigham Young University. He is the author of seven books, including *Immanent Grace, Rube Goldberg Machines: Essays in Mormon Theology, Speculative Grace, Letters to a Young Mormon,* and *The Gospel According to David Foster Wallace: Boredom and Addiction in an Age of Distraction* (forthcoming). He is co-editor, with Joseph Spencer, of the series *Groundwork: Studies in Theory and Scripture*, published by the Neal A. Maxwell Institute for Religious Scholarship, where he serves as the director of the Mormon Theology Seminar.

It's tempting to take everything personally. And then, having taken it personally, to keep it.

It's tempting to read everything as a sign and to see the whole world as a coded message: the people, the plants, the rain, the traffic, the rocks, the books, the stars, the furniture. Treating the world as a code, I can take it all personally. Things that look to be about anything but me can, once the code is cracked, reveal that I was, all along, at the center of things. Everything is a sign and these signs all point in the same direction: me. If things line up in my favor, it's a sign that, as I suspected, I'm better and more important than everyone else. And if things line up against me, it's a sign that, as I suspected, I'm broken or worse.

Rain on your run? Passed over for promotion? Rabbits in your garden? Belt too tight? Traffic when you're late? Dishes in the sink?

Woman with a blouse too sheer? Asthma in the summer? Stain on your tie? Kids fighting over toys? Husband lazing on the couch? Craving for sugar? Bored at church? Transmission failing? Horny? Dear God, why *me*!

With this kind of myopia, nothing ever gets to just be whatever it is. Rain is never just rain. Kids are never just children. Traffic is never just cars. Everything is an affront. The whole world has to be read like tea leaves. Everything has to become something else. Everything has to be a means to something else. Everything has to be a sign. Everything has to get taken personally. The whole world has to get taken and arranged around my own proper person so that it can become proper to me. The whole world must become property. When everything becomes a sign and everything becomes transferable, then I can own it all.

Having strapped the world to my back, I bear the burden of it. The more stuff I take personally, the more stuff I claim as my own, the more things I try to keep and control, the further my ambition reaches, the heavier life becomes. I carry the weight of a thousand expectations the world can never meet, and then despise the world for leaving them unmet. Taking every gain and every loss personally, I lose both the world and my own person. Claiming everything for myself, I never am just whatever I am.

There is panic fueling this drive to take everything personally and then, having taken it all, to keep it. But the world, even if it could be claimed, can't be kept. The world is passing away and this passing can't be stayed. Everything that has been given will be taken away. Everything that you've tried to own will have to be returned. To see the world with open eyes is, as Hugh Nibley said, to see the world "involved in a huge ceaseless combustion, a literal and apparent process of oxidation which is turning some things slowly, some rapidly, but all things surely to ashes."[1]

My awareness of this passing, however buried, is what motivates both my frustrated denials and my hunger for acquisition. But time is the rule: what is given can be received but it can never be kept.

Religion reveals the truth about time. Religion means to reconcile me to this truth by putting an end to my search for signs. In place of sign seeking, religion urges faith. It urges me, rather than taking everything personally, to trust things to be what they are. This reconciliation is accomplished by way of sacrifice: where time reigns, the law of sacrifice is imposed. The law of sacrifice doesn't require everything be immediately lost or destroyed, but it does require that *my claim* to everything be relinquished. All of my property, everything I hoped to make proper to me, everything I wanted to take personally, must be surrendered.

But such surrender isn't the end. Once sacrifice is offered, an inversion ensues. No longer trying to keep what is given, I become capable of receiving it. Having yielded my life, I become finally capable of living.

There's no way around the necessity of sacrifice. "Let us here observe, that a religion that does not require the sacrifice of all things, never has power sufficient to produce the faith necessary unto life and salvation."[2] The world is going to pass either way. There is no third choice. The law of sacrifice asks us to let that world pass willingly. It asks us to willingly affirm the world's passing as the condition for our living in it and belonging to it. When I become indifferent to what the world seems to mean for me, when I cease to take everything personally and sequester the sum of it as property, only then do I become capable of caring for what it is.

The law of sacrifice is the law of the gospel. When this law is lived in whole rather than in part, Mormons call it the law of consecration. The law of consecration requires that everything be sacrificed: our property, our talents, our time, our lives. Consecration is a way of sacrificing life for the sake of life. Consecration is a way of holding the world as it passes away. It is a way of returning all we're given before it is again taken from us. It is a way of receiving with care and attention what is actually given, as it actually is, for however long it actually lasts, rather than demanding that it be something else.

The law of consecration is a way of enacting the end of the world before the end arrives. It enacts a future eschatology in the present tense. Rather than waiting for endings, for bitterness, the law of consecration preemptively sacrifices any claim I may have on the world in order to open space on the far side of that loss for the world's reception. The law of consecration frees the world for care. Consecration liberates the world from ownership and then, beyond the bounds of property, returns us to it as stewards. By bringing my dubious claims to ownership to a premature and necessary end, I am saved. No longer locked up as property, life can breathe, circulate, and pass. Already returned, the time that remains for each is a blessing, rather than a curse.

This space—this time between our preemptive return of the world and that world's passing away—is Zion. Zion is a name for the world seen from the perspective of that world's passing away. Zion is a name for the world sacrificed as an act of consecration. Zion is a name for the world opened to us by our willingness to let it go. It names a world that is available for our use and care because we no longer claim ownership.

Or, as Joseph Smith puts it in section 97 of the Doctrine and Covenants, Zion is the pure in heart.

> And the nations of the earth shall honor her, and shall say: Surely Zion is the city of our God, and surely Zion cannot fall, neither be moved out of her place, for God is there, and the hand of the Lord is there; and he hath sworn by the power of his might to be her salvation and her high tower. Therefore, verily, thus saith the Lord, let Zion rejoice, for this is Zion—THE PURE IN HEART; therefore, let Zion rejoice, while all the wicked shall mourn.[3]

While the wicked mourn the world's passing, Zion rejoices. Having already and preemptively accomplished the world's end by way of sacrifice, Zion rejoices in the fact that still the world remains. While the wicked groan beneath the weight of superimposed signs, Zion delights in the freedom that arrives in letting things be. Zion is the pure in heart. A pure heart is a heart that has stopped taking everything personally. A pure heart is a heart that has stopped trying to keep everything by keeping it from passing away.

The widow of Zarephath models this act of consecration. She, a widow, has seen firsthand the world's passing. Now her time is near. The earth is baked and rainless. The land perishes from hunger. God sends Elijah and Elijah asks for "a little water in a vessel" and "a morsel of bread" to sustain him. She responds: "As the Lord thy God liveth, I have not a cake, but an handful of meal in a barrel, and a little oil in a cruse: and, behold, I am gathering two sticks, that I may go in and dress it for me and my son, that we may eat it, and die." The widow and her son are going to die. Their passing can be postponed only for a moment by the handful of meal that remains. But rather than taking Elijah's request (or her meal and oil) personally, she preemptively sacrifices them both. She makes a little cake for Elijah and feeds him. She refuses to postpone her passing and consecrates everything that's left. And then, having relinquished her claim to the world, God returns the world to her. Miraculously, for all the time that remained before her death did finally arrive, "the barrel of meal wasted not, neither did the cruse of oil fail."[4]

Having sacrificed everything, everything that remained was a joy, a gift, an excess. The empty barrel overflowed. This is Zion. The widow saw it. Her heart was pure. She entered Zion, that space on the far side of sacrifice and consecration. Having sacrificed all that was proper to her own life, God filled her with the power to start living that life. God showed her a world in which everything—including herself—was free to be just whatever it was. Everything that happened after was a grace.

NOTES

1. Hugh Nibley, "The Way of the Church" in *Mormonism and Early Christianity* (Salt Lake City: Deseret Book, 1987), 303–304.

2. N. B. Lundwall, comp., *Lectures on Faith* (Salt Lake City: Bookcraft, 1999), 6:7.

3. See Doctrine and Covenants 97:19–21.

4. See 1 Kings 17: 10–16.

Finding Zion Abroad
by Shawni Eyre Pothier

SHAWNI grew up with stars in her eyes about mothering, and also about traveling the world. Right now she is living her dream with her husband and five children in China. Shawni has found so much joy in the journey of motherhood and loves to share that joy with others through her blog at 71toes.com. Her youngest child, a daughter named Lucy, was born with a rare genetic syndrome that causes blindness. Shawni feels that although this diagnosis has been heart-wrenching in so many ways, Lucy has been an amazing blessing in their family and has taught them to appreciate all the little things life has to offer. With writing as one of her biggest passions, Shawni and her mother co-authored a book called *A Mother's Book of Secrets*. In 2011 she had the honor of being named the National Young Mother of the Year by American Mothers Inc. and has enjoyed presenting and meeting wonderful mothers all over the world.

M y five children surround me, wind toying with their hair, bright smiles stretched across their faces as historical landmarks whiz by, creating blurred lines of color.

We are riding motorbikes through the streets of Vietnam, learning history never covered in textbooks, fascinated by another new culture. We are surrounded by people so different from us yet so much the same.

We are living in China for a semester (and are on a side trip to Vietnam). Some opportunities with my husband's work have invited us to leave the comfort of home where we have lived for thirteen years snuggled securely in the desert of the American West, to embark on an adventure in the East. The adjustment for some of our children has been a rollercoaster. They are missing a lot at home. But my husband and I, in our deliberation on whether or not to make this trip happen, knew the wealth of experience waiting in this foreign land would far outweigh anything missed back home.

We were right. We are all learning more than we bargained for.

What we didn't anticipate was how much our own little corner of "Zion" would grow while we're here. *I believe that "Zion" is to be found in building strong families.* And I believe, on this foreign adventure of ours, we are building ours more deliberately than ever before.

Sure, that can be done at home. People build their own forms of modern-day Zion in every corner of the earth, whether it's in places they are familiar with or not. But for me, living abroad without all the distractions of home seems to make it easier to focus on my family. And I am so grateful.

Once upon a time, in a land far away, a young teenager left her own comforts of home to live with her family in London for six months.

That shy girl thought she would surely die.

She had scarcely begun to make friends in high school and was as insecure as they come. She had to wear a gloomy brown school uniform every day to her musty, dark, and lonely high school (at least that's how it seemed to her). But that girl and her family grew by leaps and bounds on that trip. They plowed through travel books and museums. They split up on airplanes and learned to talk to new people. They stretched out like ducks in a row, running to keep up with their parents to catch trains while lugging suitcases behind them. The more they traveled the more they bonded, and the more their horizons were stretched out before them. And that girl? Well, she looked back on that trip as a defining time for her, as well as for her family. So defining, in fact, that she sought to recreate it for her own family one day.

How do I know all this?

Well, I am that girl. That shy, inconsolable girl was me. I firmly believe doing that hard thing helped define who I am. It helped define what I wanted to become. And surely, built our own little Zion in our family as we depended on each other and clung to each other like never before. I consider that trip to be one of the biggest reasons we are all such bonded adults.

In the scriptures, Enoch's people were called Zion because they were "of one heart and one mind, and dwelt in righteousness; and there was no poor among them"[1] We have found it interesting how, as a family, leaving the extracurricular distractions behind in the states has helped us become more "of one heart and one mind."

Just because we are in a foreign land doesn't mean we are miraculously "dwelling more righteously." Unkind words still fly, the kids get annoyed with each other, there are moody afternoons coupled with bouts of homesickness. But we also each feel needed to lift one another and shine our lights in a new unfamiliar land. We have never been as united as a family.

Since the youth theme[2] was introduced a few years ago incorporating Doctrine and Covenants 115:5 6, it has become one of my favorite scriptures: "Verily I say unto you all: Arise and shine forth, that thy light may be a standard for the nations; And that the gathering together upon the land of Zion, and upon her stakes, may be for a defense, and for a refuge from the storm, and from wrath when it shall be poured out without mixture upon the whole earth."

I love the word *Arise*. I love that it is an action word. Of course you can arise and build Zion anywhere you may be in the world. We have felt the need to arise more than ever thrown into the unfamiliar; our senses and awareness are heightened. Family scripture study has become more meaningful. Family prayers are more focused. The way we reach out and help each other is more pronounced.

I'm not saying Zion is to be found lugging your family overseas. Far from it. You can arise and build Zion anywhere you may be in the world. Zion is to be found in nurturing and reworking and making changes that let us build strong families, and to help those families arise in whatever capacity they can. Living in a foreign land magnifies my ability to arise—in some sense, it forces it. For others, making a simple change, like stronger family prayer or more deliberate family dinners, can change the trajectory of family bonding. Seeds of Zion sprout and intertwine to create strength and beauty. We are all raised differently. We all seek for goodness in our own unique ways. We all have our own paths to find and iron rods to cling to. Whatever those paths may be, we must let our ear be listening to the call to "Arise" and we must take action to follow the call.

And as I watch my children this afternoon in Vietnam, one son followed by four daughters, I picture them projected into the future. I hope the bonds we are establishing, whether in a foreign land or tucked back at home, will hold them together as they set off to create their own corners of "Zion." Whether a brother or sister, aunt or parent, we all have our parts as members of families to grow strong and enlightened ones, in whatever way we can.

Strong families are the building blocks of Zion all over the world.

NOTES

1. Moses 7:18, Pearl of Great Price.

2. Every year, the church chooses a theme for the youth program, which encompasses young men and young women ages twelve through eighteen. In 2012, the theme was "Arise and Shine Forth," which quoted in Doctrine and Covenants 115: 5. See https://www.lds.org/callings/young-women/messages-from-leaders/messages-from-general-young-women-leaders/news-and-announcements/2012-mutual-theme?lang=eng.

Other Branches: Zion in Community of Christ
by John C. Hamer

JOHN HAMER is president of the Sionito Group of Charities and is on the Pastor Team of the Community of Christ congregation in downtown Toronto, Canada. A past president of the John Whitmer Historical Association, John has produced maps for the LDS Church Historian's Press, Herald Publishing House, Greg Kofford Books, the Journal of Mormon History, Mormon Historic Studies, the JWHA Journal, and Restoration Studies, among others. John's ancestors joined the early church seven generations ago in 1833, and his own family history is intertwined with many expressions of the Restoration (Brighamites, Josephites, Rigdonites, Whitmerites, and Strangites). John's research focuses on divergent groups of the Mormon restoration. He is the co-editor of *Scattering of the Saints: Schism within Mormonism* and co-author of *Community of Christ: An Illustrated History.*

Beloved Community of Christ, do not just speak and sing of Zion. Live, love, and share as Zion: those who strive to be visibly one in Christ, among whom there are no poor or oppressed.

–Words of Counsel[1] presented to the church in 2013 by Stephen M. Veazey, Prophet of Community of Christ

Members of Community of Christ are obsessed with Zion. That may come as a surprise to anyone not particularly familiar with our church. Community of Christ and The Church of Jesus Christ of Latter-day Saints both trace their origin to the "Church of Christ" organized in upstate New York by the prophet Joseph Smith Jr. and five other members on April 6, 1830. Building up the Kingdom of God on Earth was the core of the early church experience as members built up communities in Kirtland, Ohio, in Independence, in Far West, in Adam-ondi-Ahman, Missouri, and finally in Nauvoo, Illinois. After Joseph's 1844 martyrdom, the cause of Zion inspired the early members who followed Brigham Young to continue to strive to build up the Kingdom in the mountains of the West. The call of Zion also inspired the hearts of the early members who chose not to follow Brigham Young west, and instead remained in the Midwest and "reorganized" themselves around the leadership of Emma Smith and her sons.

Under Emma's son, Joseph Smith III, members of the Reorganized Church of Jesus Christ of Latter Day Saints (RLDS, later renamed the Community of Christ) often interpreted the call of Zion quite literally. The city of Zion, the New Jerusalem, would still be built according to the founder's vision at Independence in Jackson County, Missouri. Learning from the failure of his father and other early church members to redeem Zion militarily in 1834, Joseph III taught instead the Peaceable Kingdom of Zion would only be redeemed peacefully. The young RLDS Church adopted "Peace" as its motto, and for its flag and seal took up Isaiah's image of the Peaceable Kingdom: the lion laying with the lamb and a child.[2] The early RLDS settlement and church headquarters was called Lamoni, in honor of the Book of Mormon's pacifist Lamanite king, but near the end of a long life, Joseph III fulfilled his father's dream of redeeming Zion by moving the RLDS Church to Independence, Missouri.

Through RLDS vision and faith, Zion has expanded far beyond a literal conception. A temple was built in Independence, Missouri, fulfilling the vision of the prophets, but Joseph Smith III's son and successor, Frederick Madison Smith, called members to build Zion in their own communities. By creating institutions like schools, hospitals, orphanages, and senior housing, along with agricultural and industrial cooperatives, Zion would become a reality. Members became so focused on Zion that we coined the term "Zionic" to describe our many community-building initiatives.

That Zionic focus has endured into the twenty-first century. Changing our name—from Reorganized Church of Jesus Christ of Latter Day Saints to Community of Christ— reflects our focus on building communities of Christ, literally "building Zion." This is our mission as a church and aspiring to live as Zion is our identity. This focus is reflected in Community of Christ's five "Mission Initiatives"—a mission statement similar to the mainstream LDS Church's "Four-fold Mission of the Church." Community of Christ's Mission Initiatives are: (1) Invite People to Christ, (2) Develop Disciples to Serve, (3) Abolish Poverty, End Suffering, (4) Pursue Peace on Earth, and (5) Experience Congregations in Mission.

Community of Christ's Mission Initiatives is our blueprint for building up the Peaceable Kingdom of Zion on Earth in the twenty-first century. We aspire to bring everyone into inclusive communities of Christ, where all are empowered regardless of gender, race, ethnicity, sexual orientation, economic circumstances, and the like. In developing disciples to serve, we uphold the early Restoration ideal of continually learning and growing in education, experience, and wisdom as core to Kingdom-building. Jesus taught "Blessed be ye poor: for yours is the kingdom of God" and we therefore see the goal of abolishing poverty and ending suffering as crucial to achieving Zion on Earth.[3] Equally crucial is the pursuit of peace and justice, as the vision of Zion is the vision of the Peaceable Kingdom. The initiative of "Experiencing Congregations in Mission" is the aspiration to experience Zion in community together; it's the only way.

As with any faith community, the individual practical application varies widely among members. While our cousins in the LDS Church have achieved a great degree of centralization through a focus on leadership and through correlation of materials, individuals in Community of Christ are more broadly encouraged to follow the call of personal inspiration in extremely diverse ways as the Spirit prompts. In the Community of Christ edition of Doctrine and Covenants 162:1, we are called as church not simply to be a "people with a prophet," but rather to be a "prophetic people."

Unity in diversity is one of the enduring principles of Community of Christ, and we celebrate our diversity—and faithful disagreement with each other—as a strength. While I myself do not (and cannot) speak for my denomination as a whole, I can explain what building Zion in the twenty-first century kingdom means for me in my own community.

I am an active member of the downtown Toronto, Canada congregation of Community of Christ where I serve on the Pastor Team, which is equivalent to being in the bishopric of an LDS ward. Like our cousins in the LDS Church, Community of Christ has a lay ministry or priesthood. I hold the office of elder in the Melchisedec[4] priesthood, which means the primary focus of my ministry is inviting people into our community in order to build up Zion. This calling poses a special challenge in our extremely cosmopolitan setting. A majority of Toronto's residents are immigrants, drawn from all over the world. Although there is a vast diversity of religious background— as some Torontonians may have grown up Christian, others Muslim, Buddhist, Hindu, and more—a majority have become unchurched and disconnected from any organized religion. As such, many in the city have little more than a superficial familiarity with Christianity. The task of translating the value of the gospel is consequently complex and difficult. Nevertheless, I've found the idea of Zion can be translated and shared among diverse people; many feel the desire to live life meaningfully but simply lack a network or community to help achieve that goal.

Our congregation has helped found and develop additional institutions to apply our Mission Initiatives in our own neighborhoods. One of these projects is the Encounter World Religions Centre. Taking advantage of Toronto's incredible religious diversity, EWRC invites people to learn of other faiths. In the classroom, religious studies professors present participants with information on the history, beliefs, and practices of individual faith traditions. This is then followed with visits to houses of worship of other traditions. This year, the Encounter group visited a Native American lodge, a Zoroastrian temple, a Zen

Buddhist temple, a Chinese Buddhist temple, a Daoist temple, three different Hindu temples, a Sunni mosque, an Orthodox Jewish synagogue, a Reform Jewish temple, a Sikh gurdwara, a Rastifari center, a Wiccan center, a Greek Orthodox Church, and a Catholic cathedral. It was amazing how much there is to learn in leaving the classroom and actually meeting members of other faiths. There is no better way to overcome our own biases than through learning about other traditions and meeting people whose beliefs and practices differ from our own.

Another of our Toronto missions is working to abolish poverty. Poverty and homelessness are serious problems, as in all cities across North America. For decades our congregation has provided subsidized housing for people with limited incomes, many of whom struggle with mental illness and might otherwise be left homeless. I currently serve as president of the Sionito Group of Charities, which operates three apartment buildings serving over a hundred residents in the city. "Sionito" is Spanish for "a little Zion"—it's the name Latin American refugees gave to the charity's first apartment building in Toronto. The second building was named "Zerin" after the mountain moved by faith alone by the brother of Jared in the Book of Mormon.[5] The names Sionito and Zerin continually remind us that while our goal of "Abolishing Poverty" seems impossible, with faith we can accomplish anything.

It is with that faith members of my congregation in Toronto and in other Community of Christ congregations around the world are continually seeking to build a Sionito—a little Zion—here and now in the twenty-first century. Jesus taught that the Kingdom of God is at hand and we believe it is present among us when we build Zionic communities in Christ's name.

NOTES

1. "Word of Counsel" is a phrase Community of Christ members give to revelations presented to the World Conference by the president of the church in his role as prophet, seer, and revelator to the church. The conference, which is made up of representatives from the church's Mission Centers (dioceses or districts), prayerfully ponders the Words of Counsel to decide whether the inspired document should be added to the canon of scripture as a new section of the Community of Christ Book of Doctrine and Covenants. The 2013 Words of Counsel will likely become Doctrine and Covenants 165 at the next World Conference in 2016.

2. Isaiah 11:6.

3. Luke 6:20.

4. Community of Christ and the LDS Church both emerged out of the broader Restoration tradition in North America, which includes the Stone Campbell Movement (including the Churches of Christ and Disciples of Christ). The tradition sought to "restore" the early Christian church by adhering as closely as possible to New Testament precedents. Leadership was held by a lay ministry ordained to priesthood offices mentioned in scripture, including teacher, priest, and elder. Under the leadership of Joseph Smith Jr., our portion of the tradition diverged radically from other Restorationists as a much more elaborate system of priesthood orders and offices emerged. In these later developments, the office of elder became seen as part of the Melchisedec priesthood (spelled "Melchizedek" in the LDS Church), along with the offices of high priest, evangelist ("patriarch" in the LDS Church), seventy, apostle, and prophet. The offices of deacon, teacher, and priest became seen as part of the Aaronic priesthood. Priesthood ordination in Community of Christ is completely open to women and men without discrimination based on sexual orientation.

5. See Ether 12:30, or 5:30 Community of Christ.

How They Eat in Heaven
by Kathryn Lynard Soper

KATHRYN is author of the memoir *The Year My Son and I Were Born* and founding editor of *Segullah: Writings by Latter-day Saint Women*. She has edited four published anthologies of narrative nonfiction, and has contributed to Mormon forums from *Meridian Magazine* to *Sunstone* on a variety of topics including gender issues, disability, mental health, sexuality, family life, and spirituality.

I. Ten minutes before Sacrament meeting was scheduled to begin, Reed burst into the kitchen wearing his dark suit and an air of frustration. "What's wrong?" I asked, pajama-clad, washing the thermometer for one of the sick kids.

"There's no bread," he said as he rummaged through the cupboard. "Last week was General Conference and the teachers' quorum presidency forgot to make the assignment. None of the advisors are at church yet, so the bishopric gets to fix the problem." He shut the door and opened the freezer. Grabbing a frozen loaf, he shoved it into the microwave and set the defrost timer, then looked at his watch and shook his head.

I peeked out the front window, where I could see my fourteen-year-old son and his friend in the backseat of Reed's car, looking only slightly sheepish.

When the timer beeped, Reed retrieved the bread and tucked it under his arm. Although exasperated, he paused to kiss me on his way out. "Good luck," I said.

He rolled his eyes and forced a smile, then headed for the door.

II. A man spoke with God about heaven and hell. God said to the man, "Come, I will show you hell."

They entered a room where a group of people sat around a huge pot of stew. Everyone was famished, desperate, and starving. Each held a spoon that reached the pot, but each spoon had a handle so much longer than their own arm that it could not be used to get the stew into their own mouths. The suffering was terrible.

"Come, now I will show you heaven," God said after a while. They entered another room, identical to the first—the pot of stew, the group of people, the long-handled spoons. But there everyone was happy and well-nourished.

"I don't understand," said the man. "Why are they happy here when they were miserable in the other room and everything was the same?"

III. The high school auditorium was dark and filled to capacity with fidgeting students, glad to have an excuse to miss class. I slumped in my seat in the sophomore section, contemplating a nap. Didn't seem likely. Three enormous screens had been placed at the front of the auditorium along with towers of stereo speakers, and the principal was commanding our attention on stage.

"We're pleased to share with you today a special multimedia presentation titled *The Gift*."

For the next half-hour the screens flashed in rapid succession, forming familiar scenes: kids at school, opening books and lockers and soda cans; kids with troubled faces and jeering faces, kids banded together in tight groups with pointing fingers and kids sitting alone, heads bowed. Voiceovers gave snippets of inner monologue which revealed that, all appearances aside, everyone is hungry—desperately, gnawingly hungry—for acceptance and approval.

I groaned silently, knowing what would be next: some kind of "come together" montage. Sure enough. Covering all three screens, a dozen of the featured teens stood in a row. The sullen girl with huge hair turned to the football quarterback standing next to her and slowly hung a gold medal around his neck, Olympic-style. Then the QB turned to the skinny, pimply guy next to him and put a medal around his neck. And so on, and so on. Kids who'd barely looked at each other before, or who'd pelted each other with derision and scorn, now freely gave each other The Gift as (what else?) Foreigner boomed through the speaker towers:

I want to know what love is . . . I want you to show me

IV. My heart pounded as I moved up in line, closer and closer to the white-robed priest holding a silver chalice. Spending the weekend with my Irish Catholic friend Erin, I'd vaguely suspected that I'd attend mass with them, but I hadn't expected to be offered communion. At age ten it had been years since I'd stood before the Greek Orthodox priest, and I'd long since grown accustomed to the Mormon sacrament. I made Erin go first so I could see what to do.

When it was my turn, the priest gave me a brief look, then proffered the spoon. "The blood of Christ," he said. I swallowed the sickly sweet wine, and then opened my mouth again to receive the holy Eucharist. "The body of Christ," he said. I thought the wafer would taste and feel something like a water cracker, crisp and melty. But on my tongue it felt firm and synthetic, like a laminated cardboard disc.

I returned to my seat and watched the others receive communion. Hungry, I wished there were baskets of rich bread chunks to choose from, like I remembered from the Greek service. But even as a ten year old, I noticed something poignant about all those people standing before the priest one by one, mouths open, being fed like children.

V. The therapist uncapped a green dry-erase marker and motioned toward the white board. "Okay, let's draw the kids in your family. Who's the oldest?"

"Elizabeth," my son and daughter said simultaneously. The therapist drew a stick figure with long hair and a skirt.

"Who's the next oldest?"

"Ben," they said. The therapist drew a male stick figure, slightly shorter than the first. Then, as directed, she drew Andrew and Christine themselves, then Matt and Sam, and finally Thomas. The row of little green heads looked like descending stairs.

"Okay. Now, who picks on who?" she asked, uncapping a red marker.

Andrew and Christine looked at each other, then started to explain. The therapist drew curved red arrows to illustrate the pecking order. Elizabeth was rarely mean, but when she was, Ben was the target. Ben was mean to Andrew and Christine, who were both mean to Matt. In a cruel reverse move, Ben and Andrew sometimes got little Sam to be mean to Matt, too. (Nobody was mean to Thomas—yet.)

"Christine, how do you feel about all this?" the therapist asked, pointing to the pattern. Red arrows of hurt shooting from one sibling to the next

Christine's lower lip started to tremble. "I feel sad," she said.

We waited in silence for her to continue.

"It really hurts my feelings when Ben is mean to me, but then I do the same thing to Matt even though I know it's wrong." She began to cry in earnest. "I don't want to be mean but I am anyway, and I don't understand why. Matt doesn't deserve to be picked on." She sniffled a few times, then exhaled. "Nobody does."

VI. There is a passage in Barbara Kingsolver's *The Bean Trees* where her characters are telling stories while gathered around a cauldron of hot soup.[1] In one story, the characters are in an imaginary hell, where a delicious pot of hot stew bubbles on the table, but where everyone is starving. You see, they have spoons which are too long, and which make feeding themselves impossible—in their own isolation, they cannot nourish themselves.

In heaven, the same pot of stew bubbles on the same table, the same too-long spoons are in hand, but instead of starving and wasting, the friends are well-fed and happy. The only difference at all between heaven and hell . . . they have learned to feed each other.

VII. Reed looked more tired than usual when he came home that afternoon. By four p.m. he'd already spent ten hours at church that day, and after dinner he would be heading back for a few more.

"How'd things turn out?" I asked. "With the sacrament, I mean."

He sighed, and then smiled—for real this time. "We started ten minutes late. What can you do?"

I smiled too, thinking of the young priests hastily assembling the slices of half-frozen bread on the stainless steel trays. During the sacrament hymn they'd have torn the white slices into bite-size pieces, and then, after the prayer of blessing, handed the trays to the deacons. One of the deacons, perhaps even Andrew, had offered a tray to the bishop and his counselors. Then the other deacons had passed the trays from row to row, and the ward family had eaten, holding the trays for each other, leaning with outstretched arms to close the gaps between families in the pews, offering each other The Gift.

I only hoped the bread had thawed soft by then.

NOTES

1. Barbara Kingsolver, *The Bean Trees* (New York: Harper Paperbacks, 1988), Chapter 7.

Imagining a Normal, Not-weird Zion Community (Or, Maybe a Little Weird)
by Ann Cannon

ANN (A. E.) CANNON was born in Salt Lake City but grew up in Provo, Utah, where she attended public schools and graduated from Brigham Young University. During a childhood illness, Ann became an avid fan of literature and gained a lifelong interest in books written for young readers. While in graduate school, Ann took an adolescent literature class that changed her life. She began writing novels for young adults and eventually won the Delacorte Press Prize for *Cal Cameron By Day, Spider-Man By Night*. She has published thirteen books, including *Charlotte's Rose* and (mostly recently) *Sophie's Fish*. Ann has also published feature articles in local and national magazines and currently writes a weekly column for *The Salt Lake Tribune*. She and her husband, Ken, are the parents of five sons and have welcomed daughters-in-law and now grandchildren into the family. Ann and Ken live in Salt Lake City with three dogs, two cats, two parakeets and one parrot.

I'll never forget a conversation I overheard in the Thunder Hole gift shop in Acadia National Park. Two employees—they looked like college students holding down summer jobs—were discussing with great gusto a group of people who (among other things) slit the throats of strangers.

Okay. Fine. I confess. As a devotee of true crime stories, I was more than a little interested. So I sidled up to a nearby shelf (the one with snow globes) and listened for more juicy details. Of which there were plenty!

Who are these people? I wondered. *Where do they live? Papua New Guinea?* Because you know how it is. Every so often someone from

National Geographic discovers a tribe that didn't get the memo about the Stone Age and how it's so over.

Then came the kicker.

"And guess what!" said one of those college students. "They can't drink coffee or tea. They can't even eat soup! It says so right there in their Book of Mormon."

I did a double take, just like a character in a cartoon. Wait! They were talking about . . . *us?*

I was stunned. I felt like I should say something. But what? I edged my way to the checkout stand where the employees stood. I cleared my throat and said, "Excuse me. I just want to tell you that I'm a Mormon from Utah. And the part about the soup isn't true."

Then I turned on my heel and left.

I didn't look back as I walked out of the gift shop door. But I like to think that both employees, properly terrified, were running for cover.

This happened in the mid-eighties. Because of the 2002 Winter Olympics, as well as Mitt Romney's presidential campaign, it's possible the average American citizen may now possess a more accurate picture of Mormons. I've also done my part to spread the news that Mormons are just normal, not-weird people, and we do eat soup.

Okay. Maybe a *little* weird. But a lot less weird than people might think.

I've even gone so far as to proclaim that we're a Big Tent Church—a church that welcomes everyone—something I long to believe with all my heart, although right now (frankly) I'm believing it less than I used to in spite of the Church's recent *I'm a Mormon* campaign. Being an active gay Mormon would be incredibly difficult, for example, and because I know and love gay and lesbian individuals, this makes me sad. The fallout from the Ordain Women movement has also troubled me because I know so many passionate intelligent young Mormon women—some of them former students of mine—who currently feel estranged from the church and its patriarchal culture.

And yes—I have to acknowledge, old resentments have resurfaced for me as well. As a young woman growing up in the 1960s and 70s, I lamented the paucity of female role models in our culture. How many women can your average Mormon name who appear in the Book of Mormon, for example? Women with their own names? I also resented the fact that the boys my age seemed to have so many more options open to them. While they played basketball in the gym and ran rapids on camping trips, the girls were stuck in classrooms receiving more chastity lessons. Seriously, I used to think in exasperation, why is everybody so interested in my virginity?

What I'm saying is in light of recent events, I've been feeling out of step with mainstream America Mormonism, which is why I want to speak *to* myself rather than *for* myself. I want to rejoice in the good gifts I've received because of my church membership.

I love the sense of community I feel as a Latter-day Saint. Mormons, of course, aren't the only religious types who find comfort and strength in a church community. This is a universal experience among churchgoers. Still, it's one of the things I value most about my Mormon experience.

In the early nineties, my husband, our five sons, and I moved from Utah to a little homogenous Protestant community in New York known as Tuxedo Park. People were friendly, partly because they were naturally gracious and partly because we were a social curiosity, not unlike the Elephant Man, whom the Victorians used to invite to tea parties so they could get a good look at him. I'll confess, I felt a little like a stranger in a strange land at first, which is why I was thrilled when an employee of one of the families in the park turned out to be a Mormon. She showed up on my front porch, took me under her wing, and helped me adjust to my new life.

Here's the thing I always say about Mormon congregations. They're like big, extended families, which guarantees there's going to be a certain amount of crazy. Just like my friend Becky's uncle, who used to show up at family parties wearing women's chandelier earrings and then proceeded to photobomb everybody's pictures, you're always going to have those ward members who make you want to die of sympathetic embarrassment whenever he or she speaks in a church meeting. And yet somehow you become deeply connected with people you might never choose as friends. That's the beauty of it all. It's good for people to belong to people with whom they have nothing in common except genes—or core values. One's ability to empathize increases.

Another reason I cherish being an active Mormon: the opportunities the church provides for service. A friend of ours who left the Mormon world many years ago confessed he misses the service part most. Turns out he's not very good about finding and following through with those opportunities on his own.

I learned a lot about service from a woman in our ward named Sharon Kamerath, who caused me to revisit the New Testament story about two sisters, Mary and Martha. Martha was practical while Mary was a dreamer. When Jesus visited their home, Martha bustled about taking care of her guests while her sister sat at Jesus' feet and listened to him teach. Predictably this annoyed Martha. She needed Mary's help and she complained to Jesus, who gently rebuked her. "Martha, Martha, thou art careful and troubled about many things: But one thing is needful: and Mary hath chosen that good part, which shall not be taken away from her."

When I was younger I prided myself on being a "Mary" rather than a "Martha." Jesus himself said Mary had "chosen the better part," which I interpreted to mean it was okay to daydream instead of helping my mother with the dishes.[1]

Sharon, however, was a Martha. A Martha on steroids. When our first son went on a mission, she showed up to help at the open house that we held prior to his leaving, and by "help at the open house" I mean she commandeered my kitchen and elbowed me out. Later that week she showed up with essentials my kitchen was lacking because she knew I'd never bother to buy them myself.

Here's another way Sharon served. After sacrament meeting, she stayed quietly behind and picked up after the rest of us—straightening hymn books, throwing away stray programs.

After Sharon died two years ago, I vowed to do the same, which I don't always. But I try. Thanks to Sharon, I value the women who serve others with Martha's practical gifts.

Another reason I'm happy to say I'm a Mormon? The church culture can and does create good men. I'll bet you didn't see *that* coming, did you? But it's true. Many years ago, I interviewed Carol Lynn Pearson shortly after the publication of her memoir, *Good-bye, I Love You*, about caring for her ex-husband as he lay dying with AIDS. She said something I've never forgotten—she deeply appreciated the way the church encourages boys and men to express their tender sides in public, at fast and testimony meeting, for example, or at baby blessings.

By and large, I'm not a huge fan of patriarchy as a governing system, because I worry it's fraught with the potential for unrighteous dominion. Think Afghanistan or some of the third world countries in Africa. Sometimes, I wonder how our men would feel if they looked at an Ensign-type foldout of the church leadership and saw only female faces. But as I watched my five sons grow up, I truly valued the frequent opportunities the church provided to help them focus on the needs of others. Among other things, those boys often passed the sacrament to residents of a nearby rest home. (They were especially fond of one care center resident, Betty, who always managed to turn her prayers into epic gossip sessions. *Please bless Marva's son that he'll stop smoking. Help him realize he's breaking his mother's heart. . .*)

I am also drawn to the way Mormonism spiritualizes our world. Literally. The Doctrine and Covenants tells us that before the world was created materially it was created spiritually.[2] It lives. It breathes. Dare I say it even has a soul? And I love the way the Doctrine and Covenants personifies natural phenomena—makes them human—as it does in one of my favorite passages of scripture: "The earth rolls upon her wings, and the sun giveth his light by day, and the moon giveth her light by night, and the stars also give their light, as they roll upon their wings in their glory, in the midst of the power of God."[3]

That passage gives me chills on a lot of levels—first, because the language is so lyrical. Read it aloud and enjoy the way those words sing. But the idea behind them—that's what really slays me. The earth. The sun. The moon. The stars. I like to think these are living creations, too, just like we are—full of light and motion, glorying in the love of God. It makes everything around me, no matter how common and ordinary, feel infused with a grand kind of magic.

Finally, while certain people are fond of pointing out that the use of antidepressants is allegedly high among Mormons (Dude! We don't drink! So cut us some slack and back off!), I maintain the doctrines themselves are optimistic, buoyant even. Take the Mormon view of heaven. Sure, we believe some of the rooms in our Heavenly Father's mansion are better than others. But here's the thing. *Every room there is better than all the rooms here on earth. For everybody!* Who can resist a worldview that maintains we're created in God's image? We're just a little lower than the angels. We're here to be tested, true, but we're also here to learn and to grow, especially intellectually, because the glory of God, after all, is intelligence. And if we stumble along the road to wisdom—which all of us do—the Atonement of Jesus Christ is there to help rescue us.

Always.

Forever.

NOTES

1. See Luke 10: 38–42.

2. See Doctrine and Covenants 29:31–34.

3. See Doctrine and Covenants 88:44.

God as Artist: Reworking the Church
by J. Kirk Richards

J. KIRK RICHARDS makes contemporary spiritual artwork. His love of the textural, the poetic, and the mysterious has translated into a unique take on traditional Judeo-Christian themes. Richards is best known for his contributions to Helen Whitney's PBS Frontline Documentary entitled *The Mormons: An American Experience*; for his contributions to the BYU Museum of Art exhibit *Beholding Salvation: The Life of Christ in Word and Image*; for his work in gallery and museum shows; and for his sacred imagery, used in publications including *The Ensign* and *Liahona* magazines and in the non-denominational publication *The Upper Room*. Kirk and his wife, artist Amy Tolk Richards, have four creative children. They split their time between their home in Woodland Hills and their studio in the small town of Redmond, Utah. Richards' work is mostly found in private collections throughout the country.

Heavenly Father . . . is a God of creation and compassion.

-DIETER F. UCHTDORF[1]

As an artist, I can't help but compare the creations of God with great works of art. The best paintings, sculptures, novels, and musical compositions seem to have been blessed by the touch of God's hand. Art in its various forms has the ability to move our hearts, lift our sights, and bring us closer to heaven.

A recent exhibit at the Brigham Young University Museum of Art showcased the devotional work of three European painters: Carl Bloch, Frans Schwartz, and Heinrich Hoffman. I attended the exhibit repeatedly, to draw inspiration from each piece in the show. The painting that stands out perhaps most in my memory is *The Supper at*

Emmaus, by Bloch. In this painting, Jesus Christ sits at a table. He is dressed in a white robe. A halo of light surrounds his head. He hands a piece of bread to one of two disciples seated with him at a table. The disciples seem taken aback—perhaps this is the moment they finally recognize the man they've been talking to all day is the resurrected Lord. A flock of birds at sunset can be seen through the window above, leading the eye along a traditional figure-eight composition often used by classical painters, and perhaps hinting of the distance traveled earlier that day by Christ and his two disciples.

As an artist, I'm particularly fond of the disciple's hand on the table, which is exquisitely rendered. I love the subtle turning of folds in the robe over Christ's arm, echoing the muscular structure of his figure underneath. I love the candlelit glow on the face of the inn servant at the far right. I am astounded at Bloch's facility, draftsmanship, and paint surface. I'm envious of his control of color. But none of these things is what strikes me the most about the painting—what remains with me most is something many viewers might not ever notice—Carl Bloch's adjustments, or the changes he made.

These changes can be seen by standing close to the painting toward one side, crouching down, and looking up at the canvas. The sheen of reflected light reveals irregularities on the canvas's surface. A careful observer will note the exquisite hand I mentioned earlier wasn't successful on Bloch's first try. He struggled to find the right position. A ghost image of his previous positioning remains even in the finished painting. In fact, there's a ghost image of the entire tabletop, which seems to have been lower than Bloch ultimately wanted. He moved the top of the table up as the painting progressed. Similar shifts can be seen within the disciple on the left—ghost images suggest a search for form and position in the red robe and the hand holding the knife.

Was Bloch able to finish the painting to his own liking? It's not uncommon for artists to succumb to deadlines or to the demands of patrons and be forced to let an artwork go before its completion. Given the opportunity, some artists would keep a work as long as possible and make continual changes in search of perfection. The necessity of making changes throughout the creation of a work of art is a given. The very process of drawing requires the continual shifting of edges and reworking of lights and darks until nature is effectively represented or a work's poetry is achieved.

Even a painting that has undergone significant changes will be seen by viewers only in its current state. The viewer might assume that, from the very beginning, the artist intended the work to look this way, or assume the artist is happy with the piece as it looks in its present iteration. To these viewers, the painting is one thing and one thing only: what it looks like now.

Similarly, viewers, especially those on the inside, might look at the Mormon Church in its current state and assume that, from the very beginning, God intended it to look this way. If God never changes, and his principles are eternal, wouldn't his church remain constant as well? And yet, even a superficial review of church history proves otherwise. The church has changed and continues to change. Black men now hold the priesthood. Black women now attend the temple. Polygamy is no longer an acceptable practice within the church. The list goes on, from major changes to what some might consider seemingly small changes, such as the first prayer offered by a woman in general conference.[2] Like a great work of art in progress, the church continues to change.

We believe all that God has revealed, all that He does now reveal, and we believe that He will yet reveal many great and important things pertaining to the Kingdom of God. -ARTICLE OF FAITH 9

Perhaps one of the most descriptive essays on the topic of revelation and change within the church is entitled "Spencer W. Kimball and the Revelation on Priesthood." Ed Kimball, Spencer's son, outlines the events and forces at work leading up to the revelation allowing priesthood ordination to all worthy males. This article should be required reading for Latter-day Saints. As I read the essay for the first time, I was amazed at the quantity and diversity of forces at work, both inside and outside the church. I imagined God's hand in all of these forces. I was impressed with the patience of President Kimball—how he encouraged all church leaders to study and pray about the issue, and how he struggled, fasted, and prayed for consensus and unity.[3]

And in reading the essay, the thing I love most of all is that a glorious change happened. Like the moving of the tabletop in Bloch's painting, a major church policy had shifted. The church changed with God's broad brushstroke via combined top-down and bottom-up efforts throughout the earth.

I remember sitting in Sunday School with a second-generation Mormon from Ghana. A member of the class asked him, "What would you do if we hadn't received the 1978 revelation on blacks and the priesthood?" He answered matter-of-factly, "I wouldn't have stayed in the church." My Ghanaian friend isn't alone. Imagine black fathers trying to foster testimonies in their growing children, yet having to explain to them that males of *all other races* had the opportunity to hold the priesthood. Imagine black mothers longing to be sealed in the temple and yet being refused temple blessings because they were born into a family of particular ancestry. Imagine pre-1978 missionaries traveling throughout the world, hoping to preach the good news to all the earth, but weighed down with embarrassingly outdated (and morally wrong) ideas within the church that blacks belonged to an inferior race.[4]

Jesus announced his mission in the temple by quoting prophecy:

> The Spirit of the Lord is upon me, because he hath anointed me to preach the gospel to the poor; he hath sent me to heal the broken-hearted, to preach deliverance to the captives, and recovering of sight to the blind, to set at liberty them that are bruised,
> To preach the acceptable year of the Lord.[5]

At baptism, Mormons covenant to take upon the name of Christ, and as Christians, we seek to alleviate suffering and to right injustice. We must change policies in Christ's church that burden our brothers and sisters with unnecessary suffering.

Spencer W. Kimball held tightly to his faith in divine authority. He wrote to his son in 1963, expressing dismay toward saints who worked to lift the priesthood ban: "These smart members who would force the issue, and there are many of them, cheapen the issue and certainly bring into contempt the sacred principle of revelation and divine authority."[6]

And yet, after 1973, it seems Kimball and other church leaders relied on the study and expertise of "smart members" such as Lester Bush, whose exhaustive research concluded that priesthood denial dated only as far back as Brigham Young, and that the premortal-conduct theory (which, in 1973, was held as doctrine by many Latter-Day Saints) developed over time as a grasping attempt to justify Young's prejudiced ideology.[7]

A close friend to Lester Bush wrote:

> [Bush's] article had played a pivotal role in the process by which Spencer W. Kimball ultimately received the revelation . . . [We] learned from a grandson that President Kimball had under-lined and annotated virtually the entire article in his own copy of *Dialogue*. While we rejoiced in Lester's contribution, others did not . . . Following the publication of the article, Lester was gradually marginalized by local church leaders. At one point I spoke with our stake president about it, and I came away with the impression that the shunning, which was subtle but destructive, came from a higher authority. Ultimately Lester and his family withdrew quietly but completely from church activity, the tragic side of "the long-promised day.[8]

Earlier this year, I sat in on a Deseret Media Company meeting in which the church company espoused this Maya Angelou quote: "There is no place that God is not. No place. In the prison, in the choir loft, on my knees, God is right there. God is all."[9]

Allow me propose this, then: God *is* all. God is in the church. God is in the church leader defending established belief. And God is also in the change. God is in the historian who mines the past to bring truth to light. God is in the excommunicated activist who continues to work for justice. God is the great artist, orchestrating compositional shifts and corrections from all angles.

I believe Mormons today should celebrate those like Lester Bush who put forth exhaustive efforts to alleviate suffering and bring needed change to the church. Bush and others gave themselves as sacrificial lambs to give us a gospel less tainted by prejudices of the past.

The church is in a time of change. In the words of Gordon B. Hinckley, there *is* "agitation"[10] for progress. Of course, we have brothers and sisters actively involved in this agitation. I hope we'll embrace them. I hope Zion's tent will be larger than ever. I hope we won't fear change or shun those who advocate allowing God his brushstrokes.

The Supper at Emmaus is an apt painting to depict our sometime blindness. The two disciples didn't realize at first with whom they were conversing. As Latter-day Saints, we increasingly preach obedience with a tendency to turn a blind eye to the fact that Jesus Christ was persecuted and killed as an advocate for change, as was Joseph Smith Jr. Perhaps if we sit at the table long enough, we may come to recognize that those among us who work for change and to alleviate suffering are true practitioners of the gospel of Jesus Christ.

NOTES

1. Dieter F. Uchtdorf, "Happiness, Your Heritage," General Conference 2008, accessed October 12, 2014, https://www.lds.org/general-conference/2008/10/happiness-your-heritage?lang=eng.

2. Jean A. Stevens offered the benediction to the first session in April 2013, making her the first woman ever to pray in General Conference.

3. Edward L. Kimball, "Spencer W Kimball and the Revelation on Priesthood." *BYU Studies* Vol. 47:2 (2008): 44–46.

4. "Race and the Priesthood," Gospel Topics, (accessed 10/1/2014, https://www.lds.org/topics/race-and-the-priesthood?lang=eng).

5. See Luke 4:18–19.

6. Edward L. Kimball, "Spencer W Kimball and the Revelation on Priesthood." *BYU Studies* Vol. 47:2 (2008): 28.

7. Kimball, "Spencer W Kimball and the Revelation on Priesthood," 27.

8. Gregory Prince, "The Long-Awaited Day," By Common Consent (accessed 9/14/2014, *http://bycommonconsent.com/2010/06/08/the-long-awaited-day/*).

9. Oprah Winfrey, "Soul to Soul with Dr Maya Angelou," OWN TV, (accessed 9/14/2014, http://www.oprah.com/own-super-soul-sunday/Soul-to-Soul-with-Dr-Maya-Angelou-Part-1-Video).

10. "Compass interview with President Gordon B. Hinckley," aired November 09, 1997, (accessed 9/14/2014, http://www.abc.net.au/compass/intervs/hinckley.htm).

Zion without Walls
by Molly McLellan Bennion

Unable to locate a physical Zion, MOLLY and her husband Roy live in Seattle, Washington, a good substitute. They enjoy four children, six grandchildren and Molly's 92-year-old mother. Molly currently serves as a ward relief society president and Chair of the Board of Directors of *Dialogue: A Journal of Mormon Thought.*

I suppose I could blame law school, but truthfully, I embraced the adversarial system long before. As soon as I had ideas, I sought opportunities for debate, not as a game to win but as a tool for discovery. As a very young girl, I began sitting at the foot of my father's big brown chair in the evening as he read aloud Longfellow or Plato or Emerson. We'd discuss and argue, question and conclude. Throughout his life my dad discussed his ideas to hone them even as he worked to effect them. I was fortunate to be one of his sounding boards. Of course I learned more in those exchanges than he did.

It was only natural I would meet the love of my life in a high school debate class; we're still testing ideas together. If you and I are to be friends, I want you to challenge my ideas as much as I want to challenge yours. Teach me something. Let's learn together. I'm not much interested in a relationship with you if you aren't comfortable penetrating the superficial.

Zion is primarily a concept of refuge. High on the hill, walled in from the enemy, the ancient Jews created the refuge of Zion. Today Israeli Jews also find refuge within a community. Safety is a natural goal. Who doesn't appreciate the warm walls of home in a storm? We need a degree of safety to be free to explore life's other challenges. But physical safety is not my major challenge. I do not live in Israel, ancient or modern. I need not flee mobs attacking the early Mormon Saints. Furthermore, I cannot foresee a Mormon Zion, a righteous community with a fully actualized law of consecration, in my lifetime. It's interesting to consider the theoretical possibility but, day to day, I need a practical concept of Zion, of refuge, for the life I must live.

I seek refuge from the confusion and soul-destroying philosophies of modern life. I seek refuge from my own ignorance. I am both threatened and made safer by ideas rather than armed enemies. Materialism, prejudice, a proclivity for ease and comfort, the degeneration of faith in basic moral and ethical values, lack of respect for others, hedonism, greed, selfishness, a lack of compassion, and many other threats need to be understood and combated. I cannot physically wall myself from them. They are within, as well as without. I have no place to go; what safety there is lies in honing observational and analytical skills.

If pressed to name a physical Zion, I would name my dock, a quiet place over deep water and beneath a broad sky. The dock is not itself the refuge. The dock facilitates the solitary work of safety. There I find the peace to contemplate my questions surrounded by a natural beauty inspiring me to reach, to think the beautiful. There I still imagine conversations with my father. He tells me again not to let anyone do my thinking for me, but not to think too highly of my thinking either. Alone on my dock I'm reminded of what I can and cannot learn alone, great books and personal revelation notwithstanding. But the dock is just a temporary refuge and reminds me I cannot stay. The water beneath me and the clouds above me move on. I must too. I must welcome new information, debate from others, and opportunities to substitute good ideas for bad ones.

The current church is also not my Zion. At least in 2015, I would not find safety with any one group, however noble. In fact, church is a place of some discomfort for its limited inquiry. Fortunately I have been able to live in the inner city most of my adult life. I experience less discomfort in my urban ward community than I did in suburban or rural wards. Our manuals may not be expansive but my fellow members often are. My ward members come from many backgrounds—ethnic, political, economic, social and spiritual—and come with many ideas. Occasionally a new member attends our ward and visibly recoils at our diversity of opinion. A few fashion imaginary walls around the world they feel they can or should control. There they try to feel safe. It never works.

An element of my refuge, my Zion, open inquiry, lies in my friendships. My best friends are Mormon, Jewish, Protestant, Catholic, and agnostic. I want their truth. I want them to tell me where they think I'm wrong. I take them new books, conclusions, problems, and questions and they do the same with me. For many years a dear Jewish friend and I put our children to bed and walked late at night. We joked that we solved all our problems and most of the world's problems in the dark—real and metaphorical dark. Our walks corresponded with my first term as a Relief Society President and she was my insightful third counselor. Her fresh Jewish eyes saw solutions I couldn't see. Life challenges us to love God and our neighbors. That is so important and so difficult that we must keep our hearts and minds open to light wherever we can find it. We must get to know our neighbors, not isolate ourselves from them.

To find as much of that light as possible at Church, I practice a "defensible subversion." It wouldn't be subversive at all in a debate class or a courtroom. There it would simply be an open exchange of ideas in search of what's right. But a more open inquiry is thought a bit unusual, perhaps curious, and even a tad subversive by some Mormon Church members. Nevertheless, it is defensible because an attempt at honest, vigorous, humble truth-seeking is the best way to enlightenment. It's also defensible because history screams the perils of thought suppression.

Woman that I am, I remain the girl my father nourished in dialogue. I'm still the girl who asks questions, respectfully, I hope, but real questions. I'm the girl who injects biblical scholarship into Sunday School, who suggests women are not in the text because of sexist error. (Imagine: last week the Old Testament Sunday School lesson didn't include the prophetess Huldah![1] I had to speak up.) I'm the girl who raises real challenges of modern life whether the manual treats them or not. For instance, I recently asked a family counselor to teach a Relief Society lesson on sex within marriage. Sexual issues challenge many marriages, Mormon too, but the manual ignores the subject. Why would we not want to explore so important a reason for day-to-day happiness and unhappiness? When people are miserable in their marriages, they tend to have little energy for gospel learning.

Gently but firmly, I feel comfortable urging my fellow members to expand their horizons as much as possible before life expands their horizons too quickly, even brutally. I bring in new ideas, challenge old ones and, when the teacher, play devil's advocate. I encourage others to do the same. Next Sunday I will review and encourage discussion of Michael Austin's outstanding new book *Rereading Job* as my Relief Society President message.[2] In doing so, I have two goals: to inspire the sisters to seek excellent resources for scripture study and to consider the deep questions Professor Austin poses.

I urge the sisters to visit those with whom they are uncomfortable—lesbians, the mentally ill, the disabled, the poor, and the questioning. I send them to places where they must go in pairs for their own safety. We not only cannot find a Zion in which to isolate ourselves within our comfort zones; we shouldn't try. Though at the heart of the Christian message, that truth seems dangerous to some.

I'm still the girl who says "I can help you but you can't have all my time for Church activities." I need to be working and learning in other places and with other people. I need more input and more opportunities to test my output. I'm the girl who invites writers and thinkers of Mormonism to speak in my home. Tomorrow a non-member professor specializing in documents will share his study of the Book of Mormon as a document. It is likely to be deliciously thought-provoking.

I'm the girl honored to work on the Board of Directors of *Dialogue: a journal of Mormon thought*.[3] Dialogue, the process, is at the core of that sacred adversarial system which is our best hope of finding the truth. I'm the girl pressing to include my sisters in decision-making at the ward and stake levels. I'm the girl pressing for the inclusion of my LGBT brothers and sisters in our worship and service. I'm the girl likely to tell the missionaries or a ward auxiliary to go back and rethink a new program requiring ward involvement after members push back. Guilt and shame are too often the next step and they don't work. Finally I want always to be the girl a bit unsure if she's correct in facts, philosophy, goal, or means. I want always to be my father's girl.

So traditional concepts of Zion do not resonate with me. Perhaps that is unusual in Mormonism. Yet Mormon leaders have spoken eloquently for the unfettered inquisitive spirit. Consider these too-seldom quoted statements:

> *I admire men and women who have developed the questing spirit, who are unafraid of new ideas as stepping stones to progress. We should, of course, respect the opinions of others, but we should also be unafraid to dissent—if we are informed. Thoughts and expressions compete in the marketplace of thought, and in that competition truth emerges triumphant. Only error fears freedom of expression. . . . This free exchange of ideas is not to be deplored as long as men and women remain humble and teachable. Neither fear of consequence or any kind of coercion should ever be used to secure uniformity of thought in the church. People should express their problems and opinions and be unafraid to think without fear of ill consequences. . . . We must preserve freedom of the mind in the church and resist all efforts to suppress it.*[4]

And this from a current Mormon leader:

> Brothers and sisters, as good as our previous experience may be, if we stop asking questions, stop thinking, stop pondering,

we can thwart the revelations of the Spirit. Remember, it was the questions young Joseph asked that opened the door for the restoration of all things. We can block the growth and knowledge our Heavenly Father intends for us. How often has the Holy Spirit tried to tell us something we needed to know but couldn't get past the massive iron gate of what we thought we already knew?[5]

The idea that safety lies in a questing heart and mind makes some uneasy. But the argument for an unbridled and vigorous quest for truth underlies Mormon doctrine and should resonate. I am just one of many Church members who rely on that resonance as part of my Zion.

NOTES

1. See 2 Kings 22: 14–20.

2. Michael Austin, *Re-reading Job: Understanding the Ancient World's Greatest Poe*. Sandy, Utah: Greg Kofford Books, 2014. See essay herein, page xx.

3. For more information about *Dialogue: A journal of Mormon thought*, see www.dialoguejournal.com.

4. Hugh B. Brown, *The Memoirs of Hugh B. Brown: An Abundant Life*. Salt Lake City:Signature Books, 1988, 137

5. Dieter F. Uchtdorf, "Acting on the Truths of the Gospel of Jesus Christ," Worldwide Leadership Training held February 11, 2012.

Here We Will Sit Down and Weep, When We Remember Zion

by Jacob Baker

JACOB BAKER is a doctoral student in Philosophy of Religion and Theology at Claremont Graduate University. He writes about religion, theology, and philosophy, sometimes intertwining all three. He edited *Mormonism at the Crossroads of Philosophy and Theology: Essays in Honor of David L. Paulsen* and is currently working on a book on the concept of grace in Mormonism. He does not have a favorite food.

Ideologies separate us. Dreams and anguish bring us together.

-Eugène Ionesco

By the rivers of Babylon, there we sat down, yea, we wept, when we remembered Zion.

-Psalm 137:1

Could there be any ideal farther out of reach than Zion? For thousands of years various peoples have tried to build city-versions of it, only to have them captured or destroyed. Jewish and Christian communities have longed for it with such prolonged intensity that numerous locations—both past and future—have borne its designation: Zion was a ruined, once glorious city left behind in ages past; or it was a mountain, or a temple. Zion is simultaneously a future utopia, where the righteous will dwell in peace forever.

In the midst of seemingly eternal remembering and waiting, Mormons have found a place for Zion in the present: within the pure in heart, those who dwell together with one heart and mind. But who are the pure in heart? Where are those communities of people who willingly live side by side, who think and feel as one? Would any of us dare to number ourselves amongst these godlike beings, who dwell in the company of angels?

Seemingly the one place in scripture where Zion is a success—Enoch's legendary city—was taken by God to heaven without a trace. Yet we learn from Enoch that even (perhaps especially) such a paradisiacal association is not without its cost. Before God removes Zion from the world, he shows Enoch the immense suffering and evil among the peoples of the earth, and Enoch is filled with sorrow and bitterness. He would eventually receive a fullness of joy, but not before he was burdened with the sorrow and despair of the world.[1] Though Zion's city stood and shone, nevertheless God and Enoch wept together. Enoch had his Zion, yet the vast majority of God's children would not dwell there. In the single instance where a Zion was completed, it did not remain long in this world. In the long arc of human history, it was here and then gone. To consider Zion is to remember it, not because we were there and witnessed its departure, but because one way the call of Zion manifests itself in communities who live in Zion's shadow is through a collective memory of a Zion that was and then was no more. Zion haunts us from the deep past.

For Joseph Smith, Zion was almost all burden and little joy. The primary driving force of most of his prophetic career, Zion was everywhere in his letters and revelations, and he was far from alone among the Saints in his exuberance to build the City of God in America. The strict communitarian economics of this Zion, combined with physical exile from the divinely appointed site of the city itself in Missouri, led to failure after failure in establishing the visionary city. Later, he would love Nauvoo, but Nauvoo was not the Zion of the revelations,[2] it was not the New Jerusalem, and Joseph would be haunted his entire life by his failure to bring Enoch's city back to earth.

Of course we know Zion eventually became any stake, or geographical grouping of LDS congregations, anywhere in the world. If all Zion amounted to was a gathering place of the Saints, then this would surely be fully adequate. Yet that demanding injunction to become one of the "pure in heart," where those with "one heart and one mind dwell in righteousness," and where there is "no poor among them" remains. Virtually no place or people on earth measures up to these standards. All of us fall far short.

This certainly doesn't mean we cease to strive toward the Zion ideal. We are promised Zion will one day flourish, and it will still be a safe refuge from the suffering and death of the world. In our efforts to sincerely tap into the highest in us and build more unified, loving communities, other good things still often get built, though the City itself and its purified hearts may continue to elude us. Yet there is at least one commonality amongst all the iterations of Zion that seems to pervade all our various notions of the holy city: Zion is always mourned for and wept over.

Whether we are remembering a Zion of the past, or longing because of the relentless conditions of the world we currently live in, for the rest and refuge of a Zion of the future, to consider Zion is to mourn for it. Zion cannot be understood without some sense of the staggering abyss between longed-for ideals and present realities, of the irrevocable hope for a place of pure love and belonging and the alienation and loneliness of a wilderness where only remnants, at best, of such a place remain. Zion is that safe place of the ancient past we cannot seem to resurrect; it is that impossibly distant Eternal Shelter of the future that seems further and further away the more insistently we move toward it and understand what is truly required to build it.

In the absence of a refuge where we can love ourselves because others see us truly, and we are not shamed or injured by one another, but instead flourish together, we build cities around our own hearts. The walls and buildings of these cities are made of comfortable gods who are better-looking, more confident versions of ourselves; its streets are ideologies that drive us into separate villages of soul-numbing sameness; it is populated by fear that we cannot be acceptable unless we prove our worth over and over again to those who often also have a hard time loving us, because they, too, are flying apart to show us that they, too, deserve to live.

These heart fortifications are responsible for much of the violence and loneliness in the world. Our overt efforts to combat these conditions often result in them becoming even more reinforced. The one thing that often (though not always) breaks through when all else fails is a mutual recognition of shared suffering.

Someone I only distantly knew suddenly lost a loved one. This person was (and remains) a difficult personality for me. I almost always disagreed with him and generally find him to be abrasive, passive aggressive, and narcissistic. The virtual distance between us made it easier to think what I wanted about him, and I am sure there were many things I believed that had no factual basis. So I conveniently despised him from a distance, and he would conveniently, with remarkable precision, live up to my judgments about him. Yet, news of his family's loss erased, at least for a time, years of compounded antagonism. It's humbling, the effect another's suffering can have on us. Animosity and invincibility fall away upon being confronted with another's loss. The parts of our hearts that have been broken by our own sufferings reach out to the broken heart of another, and, sometimes openly, sometimes silently and invisibly, we weep together. We feel in those moments, as Joseph Smith was reported to have once said, the desire to take their cares and sorrows upon own shoulders, and cast their (supposed) sins behind our backs.

The mere fact of suffering doesn't always have this effect. When our hearts soften toward others because of their grief or loss, we can scarcely believe this experience is not inevitable. But it's not. There is nothing guaranteeing our empathy, compassion, and mercy. Sometimes the conditions for these virtues align themselves in such a way we feel compelled, against our natural, unthinking wills, to put aside our antagonisms. Other times, no matter the favorable conditions for forgiveness and compassion, we choose to bury these virtues, and reserve them for more worthy persons, often persons who can prop up our gods and make us feel better about ourselves. At times we feel irresistibly drawn to compassion; at other times confrontation with suffering presents itself as a choice. Unfortunately, we often choose hardness.

The work of mourning, which is ultimately the work of Zion that is most consistently present and available to us, is a knife that efficiently cuts away the outer protective shells we have carefully built to keep others away, obscuring our view of one another. At various times these shells are arrogant intellectualism, or an overbearing sense of humor, insensitivity to other viewpoints, or offensive remarks and irritating personality traits. But what really changes here? Traits we formerly found so difficult or impossible have not magically disappeared. Instead, our eyes have changed, if only briefly. These things have faded into the posturing background noise (where they were always most at home) of a lived life. Now we see our enemy truly, and as we mourn with them, they become a person we can actually love. Mourning elides space-time in this way, and takes what would have been years (if ever) of bitterly hard work and condenses it into a shared moment where time stands still and we are left with only each other. Mourning makes us real to one another, and in the case of an enemy, real for the first time. It counteracts the usual human work of cutting out caricatures of people to better serve our needs. Such caricatures are easier to use, dismiss, or even kill, than real persons. Only in suffering are we really together. If Zion is one heart and mind, a unified people, then only under conditions of mourning and grieving do we lay aside that which separates us.

Mourning is the pure evocation of Zion.

Zion is far behind us and we weep for it. Zion will not come and we will weep for it. Zion is ever just out of reach. Sometimes we tend to the poor a little more; sometimes we have more precise charity for our neighbors; sometimes we enjoy the company of the Saints a little more freely. But this is not Zion. Zion is what we weep for, not what we have built. Zion is what we mourn, not a goal to be accomplished. Zion is what must be redeemed, not a flawless utopia. Zion is here but is not the destination of our striving. In the funerary corners of private and public lamentation we glimpse a redeemed city that will stand for eternity. Where there is no mourning, Zion is fled.

NOTES

1. See Moses 7:67, Pearl of Great Price.

2. See, for example, Doctrine and Covenants 57:1–5, where Independence, Missouri, is specifically designated as the site where Zion was to be built.

"Let Zion in Her Beauty Rise"
by Luisa M. Perkins

LUISA M. PERKINS is the author several books, including the young adult dark fantasy *Dispirited*, the conspiracy thriller *The Book of Jer3miah: Premonition*, and the cookbook *Comfortably Yum*. A graduate of Brigham Young University, Luisa and her husband live in a small town in Southern California. They are the parents of six children.

In Saint Paul's letter to the Hebrews, he explains the nature of faith, citing examples of righteous men and women through the ages who used faith to secure promises from God. Paul points out the common thread in his narrative, writing,

> These all died in faith, not having received the promises, but having seen them afar off, and were persuaded of *them*, and embraced *them*, and confessed that they were strangers and pilgrims on the earth.
>
> For they that say such things declare plainly that they seek a country.
>
> And truly, if they had been mindful of that *country* from whence they came out, they might have had opportunity to have returned.

But now they desire a better *country*, that is, an heavenly: wherefore God is not ashamed to be called their God: for he hath prepared for them a city.[1]

God's preparation of a heavenly city—Zion has captured the imaginations of believers since before Paul's time, and ever after. Self-professed strangers and pilgrims have sought for "a better country" by various ways and means, some claiming celestial mandate, others invoking approval by divine right of inheritance. Even the story of the tower of Babel, traditionally interpreted as an illustration of the consequences of human hubris, can be seen as a mighty, concerted effort to pull heavenly society down to an earthly level.

These days, the popularity of dystopian novels and films may condition the casual observer to regard the idea of Zion with suspicion. A cooperative society in which there are no poor, and whose people are governed by a set of shared ideals? What's the catch; when's the other shoe going to drop? Historically, no such endeavor has ever lasted long. What sane, thoughtful person would want it to, anyway? Modern American culture tends to lionize the rugged individualist who bucks against any authority imposed by the state, and utopian enterprises have always crumbled in the face of disillusionment and self interest. Failed social experiments over the centuries—from Finland to Fruitlands, and from Württemberg to Wisconsin—give compelling evidence that Zion is perhaps nothing more than a philosopher's pipe dream.

For me, a latter-day pilgrim—a writer, wife, and mother living in twenty-first-century California—the ideal of Zion still speaks of hope. Zion's beauty thrives and grows. Zion's safety enfolds and nurtures. Zion offers peace and plenty for all. Zion requires work done with passion and vision and purpose. Above all, Zion promises an outpouring of grace—the enabling power of Jesus Christ—flowing into human society and making it greater than the sum of its parts. Because of this assurance of divine strength, despite the seemingly insurmountable obstacles of modern life, from political turmoil to environmental upheaval, from epidemic violence to drastic global inequalities, I believe Zion can and will be real.

"Let Zion in her beauty rise," begins a well-known Latter-day Saint hymn—a musical statement of intention and hope and prophecy. Zion will be beautiful, not just because there will be no poverty, no selfishness, no pride. Zion's beauty will arise when its inherent safety and balance and freedom from want will allow people to reach their highest creative potential. In her famous 1929 essay, "A Room of One's Own," Virginia Woolf attempts to address the lack of female contribution to the Western literary canon.[2] Woolf contends that since women historically had neither a private, dedicated workspace nor control over their finances, they faced almost impossible odds when it came to flourishing creatively. Give a girl those two things and some education, challenges Woolf (and I paraphrase), then step back to watch her soar.

A room of one's own: everybody gets one in Zion, along with enough resources on which to live comfortably. With an abundance of discretionary time and an absence of financial stress, the artist's mind is free to explore and express. But Zion is not to be a colony of cloistered, dreaming poets; instead, it is the home of the well-rounded and capable Renaissance woman. Each member of society may specialize; one may farm, one may compose, one may teach. But each chooses many other activities as well—sharing in the mundane burdens of meeting the basic needs of life.

These burdens, the chores that have always been the common lot of humankind, can be seen as gifts when they do not overwhelm. The cooking, the cleaning, the laundry—the inhabitant of Zion values these tasks, knowing the mental refreshment found while peeling potatoes or weeding rose beds is fertile ground for new ideas and the solutions to problems of all kinds. She is not above getting her hands dirty. She also knows that when all share in the work of sustaining life, all will have time and energy to find fulfillment through pursuit of their creative goals.

In addition to needing time and resources to flourish, the citizen of Zion requires safety. Joseph Smith said, "Any place where the Saints gather is Zion, which every righteous man will build up for a place of safety for his children."[3] Safety is more than freedom from physical danger or violence, although that's an excellent start. Safety means emotional security as well. Zion creates the nurturing atmosphere that allows each individual to be heard and accepted. It is where I am completely known, flaws and all, and wholly valued. It implies the heart-deep satisfaction of being truly understood.

I write to be understood, to evoke a deep and empathetic response in my readers. In fact, all art is an attempt at communication. The transfer of thought and emotion and experience forges that connection. On the other side of the process, though we take it for granted, reading what someone else has written is profoundly intimate. Within a book's pages is a world someone has created and peopled; entering that world is an exercise of trust. Each character reflects a vital piece of the author's self: her questions, strengths, and challenges. Here is my work, I am saying when you read my words; here is my *self*. In writing, I both find and extend belonging, which is another way of saying I write to make myself vulnerable and to invite others to vulnerability. The life of the artist therefore carries the potential for emotional danger. But sheltered within the walls of Zion, as I strive for excellence, I have hope of a receptive audience.

Zion is not Eden, the changeless place of stasis our mother Eve courageously chose to leave, with Adam at her side. Though serene, Zion is dynamic. Art demands conflict in order to progress to satisfying resolution; life demands opposition in all things in order for growth to occur. What kind of opposition will we encounter in the ideal city? Standards of excellence are no guarantee that everyone or everything will meet them. I may not be as talented or as willing to practice my art as my neighbor, and there will be consequences to both. In Zion, we will surely feel pain and disappointment and make mistakes. I may still sometimes burn the cookies or overwrite the chapter. And I certainly somehow must find a way to cope with the fact that, though we are all alike unto God, we are each unique, with different weaknesses and challenges—and different strengths and gifts.

This individuality can be likened to that of the instruments and players in an orchestra: each instrument contributing its own voice, all playing literally in concert, moving together toward rhythmic and harmonic perfection. The orchestra acts as one body under divine direction, and if even one instrument is missing, the whole will suffer and be lessened. To borrow from Saint Paul's analogy of the body, the cello does not tell the piccolo that it is not needed, and the violin does not consider itself more crucial to the performance than the tympani.

Zion, then, will be a vast orchestra of millions, even billions—a concept difficult to comprehend in our insulated, atomized society. How do we get from here to there? God's timing is His own. I don't know when the physical "New Jerusalem" will be built, but I don't have to wait for political revolution or apocalyptic reformation. I can work to create Zion in my heart, home, and community today.[4] If Zion is the "pure in heart"; if, as Tolstoy wrote, "the kingdom of God is within" us, then the potential for Zion exists right here, right now.[5]

To build Zion in my own life is simple (which is not to say it is easy), and clearly outlined in the covenants I have made with God. Today, I can give of my time, talents, and money to serve those in need. In this very moment, I can pray for the poor and seek direction on how I can act to help them. Immediately and on an ongoing basis, I can teach my children (and myself) the joy of work—of both everyday, entropy-fighting chores and the more obviously pleasurable creative work. Every hour, I can choose not to covet; I can seek to support and not tear down. In doing so, I both build Zion and qualify myself by tiny, daily increments to live there.

Which is not to say I can earn my way into the city; further, human works alone cannot sustain it. Only the grace of Jesus Christ, which saves us "after all we can do,"[6] is sufficiently powerful to allow me entry into the heavenly society and then to keep me there. In John Bunyan's *The Pilgrim Progress*, the pilgrim Christian makes a slow and difficult journey in search of the Celestial City.[7] Within sight of its glorious walls, he encounters a final obstacle: a perilous river that must be crossed. He nearly drowns, weighed down by despair at his imperfect nature. But the love of Jesus buoys him up, keeps him from being swept away in the current, and enables him to take the last steps toward the end of his journey.

The outpouring of Christ's grace aids the pilgrim's best efforts and makes the difference between eternal separation and eternal union. In similar fashion, in striving for Saint Paul's heavenly city, I can only do my best, and trust in my Savior's mercy and power to make my reconciliation full. "Let Zion in her beauty rise,"[8] I say with every faithful action and with every hopeful choice. So may it be.

NOTES

1. See Hebrews 11:13–16.

2. Virginia Woolf, *A Room of One's Own*, accessed October 1, 2014, http://ebooks.adelaide.edu.au/w/woolf/virginia/w91r/chapter1.html.

3. Quoted by Martha Jane Knowlton Coray, reporting a discourse given by Joseph Smith in Nauvoo, Illinois; Martha Jane Knowlton Coray, Notebook, Church Archives; this discourse is dated July 19, 1840, in Coray's notebook, but the discourse was probably given at a later date.

4. See Article of Faith 10, Pearl of Great Price.

5. Leo Tolstoy, *The Kingdom of God is Within You*, 1894.

6. See 2 Nephi 25:26, Book of Mormon.

7. John Bunyan, *The Pilgrim's Progress*, 1678.

8. "Let Zion In Her Beauty Rise," *Hymns of the Church of Jesus Christ of Latter-day Saints*, (Salt Lake City: Deseret Book, 1985), 41.

Adam's and Eve's Framework for Zion
by James C. Olsen

JAMES is immersed in exploring, preserving, and creating worlds with his wife, Erin Fairlight, and their six children. He also teaches philosophy and works at the Center for New Designs in Learning and Scholarship at Georgetown University. He is a cofounder of the All Good Things book club focusing on Mormon Studies, and he writes for *Times & Seasons*.

Mormons talk about Zion in many different senses, most of which share the general idea of communally gathering, developing, sharing, and partaking in everything that is "lovely, virtuous praiseworthy or of good report."[1] There is a deep, animating question, however, in both our history and in contemporary discourse regarding *how* exactly this is to be done—collectively and individually, on both a theological and a political level.

Unfortunately, attempts to work out the details generates at least as much discord as it does creativity. My recent two years in a LDS congregation in Doha, Qatar was a Zion experience—saints from all over the world and across many socioeconomic levels were brought together not only by our beliefs but by the temporal challenges of living in a desolate environment. The social and political climate at times matched the broiling temperatures in excess of 124 degrees, and the response to both weather and culture was often the same: hunker down indoors with friends and family. Participating in online and ward-level discussions, however, one frequently observed a divisive, polemical framework—especially when the dialogue revolved around the question of whether all is well in Zion or whether Zion is in need of serious, perhaps noncontiguous reform.[2] The factional lines drawn were as multicultural as the ward itself. What made my experience one of Zion, however, was the fact that the at times palpable discord and even acrimony took a backseat to love and service. I'll never forget the friendship of the family who dropped everything to care for my children for several days in the wake of unexpected complications resulting from my wife's surgery, or the small group of sisters who quilted dozens of blankets to be donated to the orphanage where my family was adopting. In both cases, the service was rendered by those who were vocally opposed to my family's position on certain hot topics.

Too often our discursive framing, however, fails to match our practical goodwill. Is the good ship Zion sinking while the crew and passengers obliviously bask in what they take to be the sunlight? Or ought we to ignore the wind and the waves, holding fast to a faith that the Master is well aware of—and in fact has set limits on—amidst the tempest that rages? This framework or way of setting up the question of change reflects the polemics of Babylon, or an evil world, rather than the Mormon ideal of Zion. It's not that we ought to be suspicious of strong positions. The difficulty is that the framework in which these discussions take place makes the valid insights of the "opposing" sides show up as mutually exclusive, precluding the possibility of "oneness" on which Zion is predicated.[3] In contrast, we ought to affirm both poles.

The project of Mormonism naturally affirms both—that is, Zion is not perfect, though it is an exalting place, especially when we refuse to rest content with the status quo. What is needed is a dialogic context that allows for such an affirmation.

Mormonism carves out a distinct position with regard to the epic theological battles waged in the Judeo-Christian tradition: polytheism vs. monotheism, priestly vs. rabbinic Judaism, esotericism vs. exotericism, and orthodox vs. reformation Christianity. It's easy to look at these battles and conclude that Mormonism takes a middle-ground approach. But far from being a spew-worthy, lukewarm reaction, Mormonism works out a distinctive way of framing the theological battles themselves. In this manner, far from being pitted against one another, the polar ends of the warring dichotomies actually become the cherished aspects of a unified tradition. We interpret the stakes in such a way that we maintain an equal and complimentary allegiance to both God and Gods, to both scripture and priestly practice, to both prophets and institution, to both hierarchy/mediacy and democracy/immediacy.

I also think Mormonism attempts to grasp the ends of two other (related) poles, both of which are critical to our attempts to build Zion: individualism vs. communalism and liberalism vs. convservatism.

Mormon scripture, doctrine, and historical experience are rife with individualistic calls to work out our own salvation with fear and trembling,[4] as well as various declarations that neither temporal nor eternal salvation can be achieved on an individual basis.[5] As an infant I received the public ritual of being given a name and blessing. While naming is an intrinsically individuating performance, I was given the name of an ancestor and told explicitly that along with this name came a heritage for which I was responsible, and furthermore I was told that the content of my life would be measured by my efforts to serve others. Beginning with my name and throughout my life my identity has been shaped by my Mormon community. In that same blessing ceremony, however, I was informed that I would one day stand individually before my ancestor just as I would one day stand before God, to give an individual accounting for my life. It was and always has been made clear that I am an individual agent and will be judged accordingly. I find the most plausible and satisfying way to understand these is not to see them as contradictory, or explain them away by indexing them to the differing historical circumstances in which the relevant statements or commands were issued, and certainly not by collapsing one into the other. Rather, we ought to acknowledge that we're commanded to embrace both the undeniable good of individual freedom and the undeniable good of community.

It's not merely that we lose out on an important good and thus impoverish ourselves when we deny one or the other. There are also real dangers associated with doing so, dangers that are prominently manifest in recent history. Forsaking community in an overzealous glut of individualism threatens a theoretically and existentially unsatisfying relativism and nihilistic despair. In today's world it's not just the cigarette-smoking, black-beret-wearing French *philosophes* and American poets who find themselves profoundly disoriented while trying to respond to our modern experience of meaninglessness. Being reduced to a cog in an economic juggernaut, being supersaturated with a nonstop entertainment regime, being assaulted with endless arrays of choices in every facet of life, being surrounded by hosts of humans with whom one has no substantive connection, observing the spotlight on scientism and its promise of an exhaustively articulated and valueless universe—the most common and most eccentric of us struggle with these and other aspects of modern life that, in the absence of strong community and cultural values, leaves us becalmed in an infinite, placid sea.[6]

On the other hand, forsaking our individual ability to choose a life that feels both authentic and worthwhile is not something any of us would easily part with today. None of us want others to determine who we marry, what we study, how we vote, or even how we decorate our Facebook page—in general we don't want our choices or the joy of self-expression constrained. Denying individual agency and rights threatens the unjust dominations that have been so prominently highlighted and battled against in the twentieth century—the host of oppressive "-isms" that have sought (and continue to seek) to build idiosyncratically beautiful edifices by forcing individual lives into prefabricated molds in order to serve as brick and mortar.

From where I sit, these goods and the real and imagined specters haunting their absence are the animating forces behind liberalism and conservatism. Partisan positions urging one while decrying the other are misguided and miss the dialectic that the LDS Restoration offers us.

This divinely inspired dialectic is best seen from Eden—the garden toward which we ritualistically return each time we pass through our temples. Mortality—and perhaps the cosmos more broadly—is structured finitely. Our context demands that we act without certainty and without guarantees—in part because our context inevitably contains other agents. Sometimes there does not seem any way to pursue or obtain that toward which we know we ought to strive. We believe in the efficacy of God's commands, we yearn for the promised blessings, and yet we don't know how to fulfill or obtain either from within our present circumstances.

In such cases the right thing is sometimes to simply (and adamantly) hold fast to the light and truth we've already been given until we're blessed with further understanding, just as, our tradition teaches us, Adam did. He remained unyielding through the vicissitudes of change and challenge and was eventually rewarded for his dedication.[7] As a church, our clinging to and proliferating temples is itself a great example of Adamic steadfastness. Temples were given to Mormons in a historical context that was and is antithetical to esoteric ritual. Note that many of our sister Restoration churches abandoned the temple either immediately or with the waves of anti-Masonism that swept the country in the mid-nineteenth-century. The climate is hardly more hospitable today; some in Europe even questions whether maintaining this sort of exclusive sacred space adequately respects a separation of church and state or merits the status of a public house of worship.[8] More importantly, it has always been the case that significant portions of our members are themselves perplexed or even unnerved by temple ritual. Drawing nigh unto other religions in the spirit of both ecumenism and public relations has only exacerbated the uncomfortable gulf the temple carves between us and other Western religions. Nevertheless, as a people we hold tightly to these practices, while waiting for further light and knowledge. We are richly blessed because of this.

My experience courting my wife is a more personal example. Shortly after we met, while in the temple I received an unforeseen and unsolicited experience. To me it was light and knowledge from beyond the veil. Rather than follow through on my intention to abandon what I considered a childish sort of crush, I ought to pursue Erin Fairlight as an eternal companion. Confusion was undoubtedly the most prominent result of this unexpected spiritual experience, especially as the circumstances surrounding our somewhat comical courtship were anything but conducive to our getting married. I had not received a prophetic revelation of what would be but only a divine insight into the seriousness of our relationship and how I ought to act. I was clear-eyed about the unlikelihood of things working out for the two of us. But I was also riveted by what I took to be genuine revelation. I conscientiously decided to follow Adam and simply hold fast to what I had been given until more light and knowledge came.

By contrast, however, sometimes the right response is precisely the one that Eve models. Recognizing the unsustainability or lack of progression in the status quo, Eve nobly strode forward into the unknown, and in doing so made our current, salvifically necessary context possible. As our current Apostle Elder Dallin H. Oaks has said, "Informed by revelation, we celebrate Eve's act and honor her wisdom and courage in the great episode called the Fall."[9] Sometimes, when the heavens are less forthcoming than we would like, we need to act on our best judgment. Boyd K. Packer, President of the Quorum of the Twelve Apostles, has articulated this point on a number of recent occasions.

> Shortly after I was called as a General Authority, I went to Elder Harold B. Lee for counsel. He listened very carefully to my problem and suggested that I see President David O. McKay. President McKay counseled me as to the direction I should go. I was very willing to be obedient but saw no way possible for me to do as he counseled me to do. I returned to Elder Lee and told him that I saw no way to move in the direction I was counseled to go. He

said, "The trouble with you is you want to see the end from the beginning." I replied that I would like to see at least a step or two ahead. Then came the lesson of a lifetime: "You must learn to walk to the edge of the light, and then a few steps into the darkness; then the light will appear and show the way before you." Then he quoted these 18 words from the Book of Mormon:

"Dispute not because ye see not, for ye receive no witness until after the trial of your faith."

Those 18 words from Moroni have been like a beacon light to me.[10]

Sometimes we simply cannot see how to act as we have been counseled to act. In those times, we need to step into the darkness with the faith of our primordial Mother Eve.

Returning to our courtship, my wife followed in the footsteps of Eve. Her moment of enlightenment came as she realized in the midst of life's chaos that she was an agent. In order to progress she was going to have to make decisions and act on her own. I will be forever grateful for the choice she made. For us, Zion came not from holding to the course or from merely acting on the liberty we were granted, but from recognizing that there was a framework that encompassed both, a framework wherein individuality became a new unity.

Whether to hold fast or to creatively move forward in the face of uncertainty and finitude, whether to play Adam or Eve, is always a difficult dance.[11] But we apostatize from the light of the Restoration and the Mormon ideal of Zion when we refuse to see the reason and necessity of both positions. This is true in our individual lives as well as our collective life in the church, particularly as we work out together how to embody the revelations given to us as a people in the twenty-first century. As the temple shows, I think the combination happens most effectively when those disposed toward one path or another come together to negotiate after the pattern of an eternal marriage. When we do, we make Zion possible—even if the complete fulfillment of Zion requires that we first walk through the wilderness.

NOTES

1. See Article of Faith 13, Pearl of Great Price.

2. See 2 Nephi 28:19-25 and Wilford Woodruff's 6 Oct. 1890 General Conference Address, quoted at the end of Official Declaration 1, in the Doctrine and Covenants.

3. 1 Nephi 2-3 and Moses 7:18 are often cited as examples of Zion, both of which emphasize the unity of the people.

4. See Philippians 2:12 and Mormon 9.27. These themes are often taken up and sometimes reinterpreted in Mormon discourse; they lie at the heart of the well-known Mormon values of self-sufficiency, industriousness, and accountability.

5. A common theme in LDS scripture and thought, this idea is most vividly embodied in our vicarious temple work on behalf of the dead. Regarding this work, a canonized reinterpretation of Malachi 4:5-6 claims that without the ritual uniting of families throughout the generations of earth's history "the whole earth would be utterly wasted" (Doctrine and Covenants 2). Similarly, Doctrine and Covenants 128:18 declares "for we without them cannot be made perfect; neither can they without us be made perfect." The Mormon notion of exaltation is a family and community affair.

6. Speaking metaphorically of our modern nihilistic age Friedrich Nietzsche wrote, "We have broken down the bridge behind us—nay more, the land behind us! Well, little ship! look out! Beside thee is the ocean . . . sometimes it spreads out like silk and gold and a gentle reverie. But times will come when thou wilt feel that it is infinite, and there is nothing more frightful than infinity. Oh the poor bird that felt itself free, and now strikes against the walls of this cage! Alas, if homesickness for the land should attack, as if there had been more freedom there—and there is no 'land'." Friedrich Nietzsche, *The Gay Science: With a Prelude in German Rhymes and an Appendix*. Oxford: Cambridge University Press, 2001, Book Third, Aphorism 124.

7. Moses 5:1-10. As manifest in our temple narrative, Adam's trait yields a more complicated, but ultimately similar, fruit.

8. This year the European Court of Human Rights upheld Britain's claim that LDS temples are not in fact places of public worship and are therefore subject to a differing tax status; see http://hudoc.echr.coe.int/sites/eng/Pages/search.aspx.

9. "The Great Plan of Happiness," a General Conference address given October, 1993.

10. From an address delivered at a BYU 18-Stake Fireside, March 4, 1990.

11. The contemporary issues of female ordination and leadership in the Church strike me as a paradigmatic example of the difficulty of—and the need for—this dance. I hope that we as a people—members and leaders—can faithfully supplicate the heavens and receive revelatory change in Zion. If that doesn't happen, I hope we're wise in how we respond to our ignorance.

Defining Zion
by Kalani Tonga

KALANI TONGA is a lifelong Mormon and a single mom of five children. She has a BA in History from Brigham Young University, and before her four youngest children were born, she taught ninth grade World Geography and coached varsity high school volleyball. She is a lover of music and enjoys singing and playing the guitar and ukulele, though she doesn't consider herself especially skilled at any of those things. Her father's family is Tongan and her mother's family is mostly Swedish; Kalani is an unusual blend of cultures, but she wouldn't have it any other way. She writes at Feminist Mormon Housewives about religious and social issues. Kalani was born in California, but has spent most of her life in Texas, and currently resides in the greater Houston area.

Zion. Growing up, I would hear this word, but did not really understand what it meant. I most often heard it associated with the early days of the church and in conjunction with the Law of Consecration[1] and the complicated history of early Mormon polygamy—with the inevitable caveat Zion could not be established at that time because the people were not ready to be "of one heart and one mind."[2] I was also taught that Zion, sometimes also referred to as the New Jerusalem, would be built upon the American continent in Jackson County, Missouri when Jesus Christ returned to earth. To be completely honest, I hadn't given the idea much further thought until a relatively short time ago.

Recently, though, Zion has been defined anew in my life. No longer just an anecdote from history or an ideal to strive for in the far-distant future, I see Zion being built daily in my life. Zion is the desire to grow together, to learn from one another, and to appreciate and embrace our differences as we find common ground to build upon. In the communities I inhabit, I see my friends and loved ones striving for Zion daily.

I am Kalani Tonga, a half Tongan/half Swedish lifelong member of the church. I am a divorced mother of five, a teacher and coach by vocation, and a feminist and aspiring activist. I regularly contribute to the blog Feminist Mormon Housewives as a writer and moderator, and through my association with the fMh community, my vision of Zion has changed, expanded, and deepened in ways I wouldn't have ever imagined possible.

When I envision Zion, I picture a place where each person feels perfectly at home. I see a society where our unique gifts, abilities, and quirky characteristics make us valuable and integral to the community, and where our differences bring us together instead of dividing us. All my life I have felt I live in the margins—never fully belonging to any group, and yet able to "pass" and comfortably associate with any community. I am biracial, so I am "not quite brown, and not quite white." I am either on the liberal side of orthodoxy or the orthodox side of liberal Mormonism, depending on who you talk to, but regardless of which descriptor comes first, I am slightly different than the norm in either direction. I am endowed, but was not married in the temple, and I am now a divorced mother of young children, so in some ways I do fit in with the other women, wives, and mothers in my ward—and yet, I don't. All of these circumstances make me very cognizant of other people who dwell in the margins, and these life experiences have shaped my view of Zion.

In my everyday life, I meet fellow margin-dwellers and outcasts often through my online interactions. Frequently, these people are misunderstood and sometimes are even disliked. My eighth grade physical science teacher, Mr. Nierste, used to say, "Knowledge of a thing engenders a love for it," and when I ponder Zion, I think about this statement. I believe as we learn about each other, we open our hearts to loving each other more, thus bringing Zion into our communities today. General Young Women Leader Neill F. Marriott spoke in the October 2014 General Women's Meeting about the idea that we carry a circle of influence with us wherever we go, and I think this idea ties perfectly to building a latter-day Zion.[3]

As I think about building Zion within my own circles of influence, my mind is immediately drawn to a project involving Women of Color within Mormon feminism. Women of Color often feel like margin-dwellers or outcasts: misunderstood, underutilized, and even disliked for being different than the norm. With this in mind, and in an effort to support, learn from, and encourage one another, several of us who identify as Women of Color within the feminist Mormon community collaborated to create a safe space where Women of Color can grow and develop together. In my mind, Zion is a place where we are comfortable being our most authentic selves, and where we experience the love, patience, and acceptance from others that Jesus Christ and God extend to us all. This space for Women of Color has been a Zion-like experience for me. Through my interactions with the members of this group, I have found although our individual experiences vary, our pain, our joy, and our need for love, acceptance, and safety is universal. When we seek to support and learn from each other, our differences become strengths, and our appreciation for each other as unique and special children of God is strengthened as well. Thus, one way in which the building of Zion in my own community is fulfilled lies in the creation of, and my continued participation in, this group for Women of Color. By learning to value and appreciate the experiences and characteristics of this diverse group of women, I gain knowledge of them individually and grow in my love for them. I feel closer to God, and I see Zion being built in my life.

Jesus Christ never forgot those who dwelt in the margins of his communities. During his ministry, he embraced women, lepers, and social outcasts, and he used his position to make a place at both the proverbial and literal table for those who were previously uninvited. Cynthia Bailey Lee, a professor at Stanford University, gave a convocation touching on this Christ-like remembrance of the marginalized, and her words moved me and further shaped my understanding of what it means to build Zion today.[4] She spoke about using our voices to magnify the voices of those who would otherwise remain unheard. She explained the LDS concept of by-proxy temple work in which one receives a slip of paper containing the name of a deceased person he or she will perform ordinances on behalf of in the temple. Using this by-proxy temple work as an analogy, she spoke about looking around in any given situation and actively taking note of who was "not at the table," or, not a part of the conversation because they either had not been invited or did not feel welcome. She then invited all to envision reaching into our pocket for an imaginary by-proxy slip of paper representing those not present at the table, and asked everyone to start speaking up in place of those whose voices would otherwise be silent. I love this idea. What an incredible way to build Zion by emulating Jesus Christ! So often, the few who have a "seat at the table"—in any of our communities, be it church, or school, or society—neglect to take into account things in the best interest of people who do not have a voice in the conversation. The temple analogy really spoke powerfully to me because when I think of Zion, I envision a place where we hold each other's interests as dear to our hearts as we hold our own, and where those with the power to enact change and inclusion reach into their pockets of privilege, pull out the by-proxy papers of those who have been marginalized, and embrace and honor those whose voices are equally important, but usually silent. By striving to be inclusive, attentive, and sensitive to the needs of "the least of these [our] brethren" in society, we begin to build Zion today.

How we accept Cynthia Bailey Lee's challenge to actively recognize those not at the table, and to make the effort to speak up on their behalf, is different for each of us. In my life, I attempt to meet this challenge by writing about topics important to fellow margin-dwellers and outcasts, even when these topics are difficult or scary. I try to say the hard things, to start the difficult conversations, and sometimes this action is met with appreciation by the general public. Other times it is met with scorn. My vision of Zion includes embracing all of God's children exactly where they stand, with unconditional understanding, making sure everyone feels welcome at the table. In order for this to occur, individual people need to step out of their comfort zones and become bridge-builders between those who see themselves as outsiders, and those comfortably inside the circle of acceptance. Having dwelt in the margins for most of my life, it seemed only natural I should embrace this role, and I have been extremely fortunate to have found incredible role models and mentors who help me build bridges, develop relationships, and promote our vision of Zion in our communities.

What is latter-day Zion? Zion means coming home. Zion is a place each of us yearns for where we feel the embrace of love, acceptance, and peace. Zion is a place where each of us experiences the joy of being loved exactly as we are, and the sense of community drives us to do right by each other and be our best selves. I think of Christ's earthly ministry, I think about how he reached out to those in under-privileged circumstances, and I believe that Zion will be achieved on earth when we seek to do the same. When we truly see each individual as a brother or a sister, and when each person is seen as valuable and necessary to the whole, only then will Zion truly exist.

NOTES

1. The Mormon Church defines the Law of Consecration as "a divine principle whereby men and women voluntarily dedicate their time, talents, and material wealth to the establishment and building up of God's kingdom." See https://www.lds.org/scriptures/gs/consecrate-law-of-consecration.

2. See Moses 7:18, Pearl of Great Price.

3. Neill F. Marriott, "Sharing Your Light," *Ensign*, May 2013, 117.

4. "'Such a Time as This,' Remarks at Stanford Convocation," By Common Consent, accessed October 20, 2014, http://bycommonconsent.com/2014/10/09/such-a-time-as-this-remarks-at-stanford-convocation/.

On Unity and Difference
by George B. Handley

GEORGE HANDLEY teaches Interdisciplin-
ary Humanities at Brigham Young University.
With a focus on environmental humanities,
literatures of the Americas, and religion,
George authored the environmental memoir,
*Home Waters: A Year of Recompenses on the
Provo River.* His eponymous blog appears at
Patheos.

When I was in graduate school at Berkeley, my fellow students and I were sitting in the graduate lounge discussing some political topic of the day. The Bay Area, of course, is famous for its liberal politics, and Berkeley perhaps most of all. On top of that, my profession of literary criticism is predominantly liberal. So you can imagine that when we talked politics, it was rarely acknowledged that another legitimate point of view might be offered by conservatives. Despite my own left-leaning politics, I remember that day becoming increasingly uncomfortable with the image of Republicans emerging. It was as if my friends were describing a cartoon, a buffoon, or a clown, but not a real person. I finally asked if any of them actually knew a Republican, and my question was met with silence.

This experience taught me something about how valuable my church life is in helping me to live with and love people who hold different political opinions than I do. Perhaps some of us imagine we are aiming for a sameness of ideas in the church, that Zion will be achieved when we finally start thinking all alike. Frankly, to my mind, that seems more of a fantasy than an ideal to which we ought to aspire. The wisdom of democracy and of councils is that great ideas are never hatched in isolation and their greatness depends on the refining process they go through when they have been debated, chewed on, worked over, and amended in a collective effort among people of good will but of different minds. I suspect, then, Zion is achievable not at the moment we all agree but when we truly begin to listen to one another.

Can people of faith be one even—or especially—if we aren't in agreement on politics? In his letter to the Ephesians, Paul exhorts us to be worthy of our vocation as Christians. We do this, he says, by "endeavoring to keep the unity of the Spirit in the bond of peace." This unity comes with work, "with all lowliness and meekness, with longsuffering, forbearing one another in love."[1] For Paul, at least, it is not only possible, but also requisite as Christians to find unity, despite those differences.

It is not uncommon today to seek and embrace a community of faith precisely on the basis of whether or not it brings one into communion with politically like-minded people. This, I suppose, is for several reasons. It is certainly a lot easier to love and serve and find joy in communing with those with whom one has more in common. Since politics can sometimes feel so emotional, so instinctively a deep part of ourselves, it helps to bypass the divisions we might otherwise create over politics. I would argue that while this might be a safer and easier route, it cheats. It cheats because the reality of human cultures is that we are incredibly diverse. If we learn Christian living and service in a context of narrow like-mindedness, we have scarcely scratched the surface of our moral duty. When we live in a society that is politically, racially, sexually, religiously, and economically divided but we don't have friends on the other side of any of those "aisles," we are part of the problem.

Another reason political unity is preferred in church might be that some see a more direct route from one's religious persuasions to one's political convictions. Some see the transcendent truths of religion as having a singular, and not a plural, manifestation in the political context. But I would argue that this only exacerbates the problems we want to fix. If we believe the problem with the world today is that not enough people believe in the right things (i.e., the things we believe in), then doing good in the world boils down simply to persuading others and presumably judging or dismissing those who fail to be convinced. The purpose of life is not to be right. It is to do and *become* good. If it never occurs to us we might be wrong in the way we interpret the gospel, we can never imagine a distinction between God as he is and God as we understand him. Our truth will always be *the* Truth, and we will have shut ourselves off from genuine dialogue, growth, and learning. It is hard enough to calm emotions over politics, but when we add religious fervor to political conviction without any ambivalence, sense of irony, or even a sense of humor, our politics become toxic and our community shrinks.

Despite the predominance of conservatives among American members of the LDS Church, the church nevertheless repeatedly refuses to dictate political positions for its members and continually encourages each member to identify political parties and candidates that he or she believes are best suited to produce a good society. Some will claim this position of neutrality is an illusion, but they are wrong. There have been rare exceptions to this, and they come on occasions when the church weighs in on issues viewed as morally important. For example, the church spoke out opposing the MX missile proposed for Utah's deserts in the 1970s, and more recently, it urged leaders to seek meaningful immigration reform and has acted to protect traditional family structures, among other examples.

I am not naïve. I am well aware this neutrality does not always translate into a church experience that *feels* politically neutral. Despite its rarity, the church's political activity has been exceedingly difficult for some members. Where the majority of the population is Mormon, we have a historic tendency toward political homogeneity. Some like to imagine that this is as it should be. It might even seem evidence of the spiritual feelings bringing us around to sameness of thought.

I see it differently. It is simply far too easy to create homogeneity out of social pressure rather than from the hard work of forbearance and lowliness of heart that Paul described. Homogeneity might be a function of our intense desire for unity (and consequent fear of differences of opinion). We desperately want to get along, so much so that when we are in closer proximity, it makes having honest and open discussions of political differences that much harder. Our tendency is to bury difference, to rush to consensus, and to fail to practice the art of graceful disagreement. As a result, the quality of our thinking suffers.

Recently a disagreement arose in my neighborhood over a proposed bus route. This neighborhood is not only predominantly LDS, but is also entirely contained in one stake (a large congregation made up of usually five to ten smaller congregations, or wards). We go to church together. We worship and serve together and we genuinely love one another. The proposal was not a major issue and most of the disagreement has been gracious. But it was especially disconcerting for some in the community to discover we are not in unanimous agreement about what is best for our neighborhood and for our children. Assuming we should all think alike can lead to feelings of betrayal and hurt and can compromise our ability to experience unity.

As a Mormon, if you lean left politically or tend to think outside of the Republican platform, you are already well familiar with the problem of living with and loving those who disagree with you politically. You already know what it is like to wonder why those you like so much, indeed the vast majority, would arrive at such different, and in your view erroneous, conclusions about politics. And you know what it is like listen to other members make offhanded comments in church that presume unanimity on policy or politician, when in fact such agreement doesn't or needn't exist. You learn to make a distinction between the gospel and its many and various and sometimes contradictory political applications. You come to accept the possibility the spirit might inspire two people to opposite conclusions and to opposite civic commitments. Hopefully you are generous enough in your estimation of others to understand good people who do good works can also be wrong about a political matter, *including you*. That is certainly the reality I have come to understand when I watch people who share my faith face off against each other in political debate, as often happens in Utah. Differences of opinion needn't be a source of stress or tension. If we remain committed to the project of Zion, differences can help us to develop the kind of character Zion requires.

It shouldn't surprise us that spiritual feelings guide us sometimes in different directions or to make different decisions. Why is it that one mission president or one bishop feels inspired to emphasize one program over another, to call some people and not others to certain callings, only to be replaced by someone new who begins a different set of choices? This doesn't spell institutional chaos. Quite the contrary. When enacted with the same spirit of love, of devotion to God and to Jesus Christ, this difference somehow creates a dialectic in which higher truths and greater good become manifest. The truth is more than your or my ability to understand it. And the truth is for all people, not for me or for my community alone.

This is why Paul speaks of the importance of lowliness, meekness, and forbearance. To be forbearing means learning to set aside pride, arrogance, or excessive confidence, to listen and learn from others, and even to learn how to love, sustain, and appreciate the good in others—especially when we might disagree over politics. We cannot declare ourselves immune from the need for and blessings of being a part of a community. When we judge this way, we falsely elevate politics above all other values, as if we can know everything essential about a person once we know how they vote. Unity doesn't come from sameness; it comes from the work of waiting, listening, longsuffering, self-questioning, and honest deliberation. Unity comes from learning, as Paul also advised, to "speak the truth in love."[2] When differences arise and our impulse is to bury our thoughts for the sake of keeping the peace, we haven't yet achieved meaningfully unity. We cannot demand or expect uniformity on politics.

As Mormon scholar Eugene England said many years ago, the practice of being a member of the church is as important to our spiritual growth as coming to an understanding of revealed truth.[3] That is why I prefer the kind of learning experience that comes with going to church with people I don't choose as my leaders and fellow members but people I am instead called to love, whoever they might be and whatever their politics. I highly recommend this kind of religious practice.

The challenge Mormons face in the church is not unlike the challenge I saw in the Bay Area. Until and unless Mormons engage in honest and direct dialogue with those who see the world differently and learn to be forbearing and meek, Mormons will achieve meaningful unity neither among ourselves nor in society. Even more problematic, we cannot rightly call our worldview fully Christian. Genuine dialogue cannot happen when secretly one harbors the suspicion one's opponent is a nutcase or is dangerous to one's faith. A Christian community is first and foremost characterized by charity for all people. Lazy tolerance for anything and everything is not the solution, nor is political apathy. We must be passionate, concerned, *and* informed, but we must also not be above self-doubt and correction, and we must be capable of identifying whatever is good and right about those who oppose us.

Jesus Christ did not ask us to be fearful or excessively defensive. He asked us to build a kingdom in which all of God's children might flourish. This cannot be accomplished alone, in enclaves, or with fences. It is accomplished by building bridges and opening doors.

NOTES

1. Ephesians 4:2–3.

2. Ephesians 4:15.

3. See Eugene England's "Why the Church is as True as the Gospel," accessed October 15, 2014, http://www.eugeneengland.org/why-the-church-is-as-true-as-the-gospel.

Afterword
by Tracy McKay-Lamb and Emily W. Jensen

While everyone's journey into faith is unique, archetypal threads wind through our human stories, drawing us together in a unified chord—we are all stronger and richer for our unique contributions. Mormons are no different. Compiling and editing the words of so many fine writers has been cathartic and enlightening. In this volume, we have attempted to distill the esoteric notion of the Mormon Zion down into a warm and vivid reality—a lived language of the heart, mind, and, most importantly, of the embodied soul.

In a recent visit to one of our temples, there was a giant spray of flowers filling a vase on a table. Each flower was so beautiful—and yet on close examination, each petal was unique—bent here or there, a curl in the edge, a tiny ripple in the textured leaf, a frill here, smooth simplicity there; the imperfect petals, when placed in the context of the flower, became perfect blossoms. Each flower was a collection of imperfection, which was then part of a greater bouquet, which in turn became a breathtaking masterpiece.

Imperfection. Bent petals. Collective beauty in God's hands.

This is the foundation for Zion; we are made perfect by allowing God to build his kingdom with our whole—albeit often bent—selves.

Being a Mormon isn't about what your family looks like, or what circumstances earthly life has placed in your path, or where your family originated. Being a Latter-day Saint begins in a million different ways with a million different lives set gently on their personal path, but it ends up with us looking at one another and seeing a reflection of God in each other's faces. Sometimes, in the chaos and hustle of American life, we can forget, in our individual and all-too-human myopia, that we are all woven together—we don't just seal nuclear families together in our temples. The utterly breathtaking goal of our faith is to seal the family of humanity together, to progress as individuals comprising a whole, and to learn to reflect God. For Mormons, salvation is a collective communion. This is what we mean when we speak of Zion.

We are still nice. We're your neighbors. We're your friends. We're still a little weird. We're mostly good—and we're usually good intentioned. We'll help you move, bring you a casserole, invite you to play games and eat brownies with our families on Monday nights. We'll send our young men and women out into the world, certainly to your neighborhood, to speak with you about Jesus. We recognize you might not be interested, and we'll try to understand. We'll offer a shoulder on which to laugh or cry, depending on your need. We'll show up after disasters with food, clothing, blankets, medical supplies, and chainsaws. It might still be odd that we try not to curse, and will opt for root beer—or sometimes, if we're feeling rebellious, Diet Coke—as our cold brew.

Happy. Odd. Smiley. All true, at times. However, we hope this collection of essays has added some depth to those simplified perceptions.

Thoughtful. Engaged. Committed. Faithful.

Zion isn't a place. Zion isn't politics. Zion isn't even an idea. Zion is heaven, right here on this earth, and we can only build it together.

Glossary

Agency (sometimes referred to as free agency): The ability given from God to choose between good or evil.

Auxiliary Organizations: Auxiliary organizations exist to assist the priesthood government system of the church. Include the Primary (children), Relief Society (adult women), Sunday School (courses of Sunday study) and Young Men and Young Women organizations.

Bishop: A priesthood office whose bearer has been ordained and set apart to preside and be in charge over a ward. Always male.

Book of Mormon: An account of ancient inhabitants of the Americas, recorded on gold plates and translated by Joseph Smith. The record purports to contain both a history of these people and the fullness of the everlasting gospel as revealed by Jesus Christ when he visited as recounted in the book.

Branch: Generally the smallest organized congregation. Presided over a branch president.

Callings: Invitations to accept an office or assignment within the church structure or the offices or assignments themselves.

The Church of Jesus Christ of Latter-day Saints: The official name of the Church.

Comforter: When Mormons speak of "The Comforter" they usually are referring to The Holy Ghost. There is a Second Comforter as well, and that is Jesus Christ.

Consecration, Law of: A historical and temple principle whereby Mormons voluntarily dedicate their time, talents, and material wealth to the building up of God's kingdom.

Correlation: A process by which all programs of the church are correlated so that teachings, organizations, programs, meetings, and instructional materials are similar no matter where one goes in the world.

Doctrine and Covenants: Another volume of Latter-day Saint scripture containing selected revelations given to Joseph Smith and his successors in the presidency of the church. Includes revelations and declarations.

Fast Offerings: Donations given to the bishop for the relief of the needy each first Sunday of the month.

General Authorities: Members of the presiding leadership of the church: the First Presidency, Quorum of the Twelve Apostles, Quorums of the Seventy, and Presiding Bishopric. All male.

General Conference: Scripturally-mandated general meetings of church members in Salt Lake City, Utah, regularly convened every April and October.

Gospel: The "good news" of learning about Jesus Christ; the principles and ordinances of the plan of happiness or plan of salvation in Mormon theology.

Heaven: The dwelling place of God encompassing the three kingdoms of glory in Mormon theology, the celestial kingdom, the terrestial kingdom, and the telestial kingdom.

Holy Ghost: The third member of the Godhead, a personage of Spirit. Often referred to as the Spirit or the Comforter.

Israel: Members of the Mormon Church consider themselves to be of the house of Israel and related to the Old Testament patriarch Jacob as his descendants.

Joseph Smith Translation of the Bible (JST): The inspired commentary on the King James Bible that Joseph Smith embarked upon in 1830, which resulted in his receiving many doctrinal revelations that are now a part of the Mormon scriptural canon.

Kingdom of God: The church; the political government of God or God's literal dwelling place.

Light of Christ: The power of Christ infused in all of his creations.

Mormon: Members of The Church of Jesus Christ of Latter-day Saints are commonly known as Mormons, which originates in their belief in the Book of Mormon. The book was named for Mormon, the prophet-historian in ancient America who is believed to have compiled and abridged the book.

New Jerusalem: The administrative headquarters of the kingdom of God in the Americas during Jesus Christ's promised millennial reign. Prophesied to be in Missouri.

Pearl of Great Price: One of the standard works of the church, containing the book of Moses, the book of Abraham, Joseph Smith—Matthew (a translation of Matthew 24), the Joseph Smith-History, and the Articles of Faith.

Priesthood: (1) The power of God; (2) the authority to act in God's name; (3) the keys to preside within the church organization; (4) a term referring to the men of the church who hold the priesthood, but this final one is losing favor in current church parlance.

Restoration: The reestablishment of the gospel of Jesus Christ through Joseph Smith in the latter days that will continue with the culmination of God's work on the earth in the latter days, including the restoration of the gospel, the gathering of Israel, and the renewal of the earth.

Sacrament: The water and bread blessed and passed as emblems of the body and blood of Jesus Christ to church members in ward or branch meetings each Sunday.

Stake: A geographical-ecclesiastical unit of the church composed of several wards and sometimes smaller branches. Presided over by a stake president.

Temple: A sacred building, also described as the "House of the Lord," in which Latter-day Saints perform sacred ceremonies and ordinances of the gospel for themselves and for the dead.

Testimony: A personal expression of one's convictions or beliefs about tenets of the Mormon faith. Usually includes expressions of faith in the prophet, the restoration of the church, and especially the Savior, Jesus Christ.

Tithing: The donation of one-tenth of one's increase (income) to the church that members are expected to give, especially if they wish to enter the LDS temples.

Ward: A geographic unit in the Mormon Church, consisting of a few hundred members presided over by a bishop.

Welfare: A program in the church administered jointly by priesthood officers and the Relief Society leaders which tries to attend to the temporal well-being of needy members and admonishes all members to become serf-reliant.

Zion: A word meaning "the pure in heart"; also a geographic location where the righteous are gathered by obedience to the gospel.

NOTES

1. Adapted from information found at http://www.lightplanet.com/mormons/daily/vocabulary_eom.htm.

About the Editors

EMILY WARBURTON JENSEN grew up in Northern Utah in the valley where her Mormon pioneer ancestors settled. She has lived throughout the Mormon corridor except for a stint in Rexburg, Idaho, which doesn't really count for getting out the Mormon bubble since she was there to attend a private Mormon university. Emily knew she wanted to be a journalist when she was thirteen years old. She graduated from Ricks College and Utah State University with a journalism degree, then set about juggling writing and editing while mommying five mostly-delightful children with the help of her wonderfully nerdy husband. She loves to ski the Utah powder, ride horseback through Utah sagebrush, sail Utah lakes, and indulge in dark chocolate on less adventurous days. Find her work at the http://deseretnews.com, http://dialoguejournal.com, and http://bycommonconsent.com.

TRACY MCKAY-LAMB is an adult convert to the church, raised in California by wonderful and loving atheist flower children that may still be mourning her assimilation into the Mormon collective. After doing many things wrong, Tracy went back to college as a divorced single mom and graduated with honors. Tracy relocated from the west coast to the DC metropolitan area for graduate school with her three children. She recently opened her heart to a new husband and his children, making one giant, beautiful, messy family. When she gets moments to breathe, Tracy paints, studies, cooks, and writes in a creative whirlwind of artistry. She enjoys fine cheese, the scent of old books, and cooking from Julia Child's cookbooks. Find her essays at http://bycommonconsent.com and http://dandelionmama.com/.